CANDIDATE

THE TRUTH BEHIND
THE PRESIDENTIAL CAMPAIGN

EMILY O'REILLY

Attic Press
Dublin

First published in Ireland in 1991 by
Attic Press
44 East Essex Street
Dublin 2

British Library Cataloguing in Publication Data
O'Reilly, Emily
    Candidate : the truth behind the presidential campaign.
    1. Ireland. Presidents. Elections
    I. Title
    324.94150824

    ISBN 1-85594-021-3

Cover Design: Luly Mason
Origination: Attic Press
Printing: The Guernsey Press Co Ltd

For Stephen, Jessica and
the memory of Howard Simons

ABOUT THE AUTHOR

Emily O'Reilly is Political Correspondent of the *Irish Press*, she has previously worked for *The Sunday Tribune*, RTE's *Today Tonight* programme, and has contributed to numerous other publications and radio and television programmes.

In 1986 she won the 'AT Cross Woman Journalist of the Year' Award for her coverage of northern Ireland for *The Sunday Tribune*. In 1987 she was awarded a Nieman Journalism Fellowship at Harvard University, Boston, USA.

ACKNOWLEDGEMENTS

The *Irish Press*, and in particular Hugh Lambert, Editor; Tim Ryan, Chief News Editor and Ray Burke, Deputy Chief News Editor.

Patricia Carr and Jeanette O'Neill who assisted me with research and tape transcription respectively.

My journalist colleagues in Leinster House and in particular my women colleagues Caroline Erskine and Maol Muire Tynan who were a constant source of good humour and support.

Roisin Conroy, Michelle Cullen and Ailbhe Smyth, my publishers and editors, who were very supportive throughout.

In particular I would like to thank Marie O'Neill for her time, understanding and care.

Finally to the many TDs, party officials and party activists, many of whom did not wish to be named, who willingly gave their time for interviews.

CONTENTS

GLOSSARY

Aras an Uachtaráin	President's Residence in Phoenix Park, Dublin
'Cute Hoor'	Familiar phrase typically used of clever politicians
Dáil Eireann	Lower House of Parliament
GUBU	Grotesque, Unbelievable, Bizarre & Unprecedented
Leinster House	Meeting house of the Oireachtas (Dublin)
MEP	Member of the European Parliament
Oireachtas	National Parliament, consisting of two houses, Dáil Eireann and Seanad Eireann
Phoenix Park (the Park)	Refers to President's Residence
H Block	High security Maze Prison for political prisoners.
Seanad Eireann	Senate
SDLP	Social Democratic Labour Party
SPUC	Society for the Protection of the Unborn Child
Taoiseach	Prime Minister
Tánaiste	Deputy Prime Minister
TD	Member of Dáil Eireann (Teachtaí Dála)
Uachtarán na hEireann	President

Introduction

The cataclysmic opening months of 1990 had left Europe's most western outpost unscathed.

The domino-like collapse of the old East European totalitarian regimes, the literal crumbling of the Berlin Wall, provoked some intellectual questioning about implications for Ireland, but principally in relation to the lessons for the north.

The so-called 'New World Order' was happening out there, perceived as having little relevance to the internal politics of the Republic.

The seismic changes in the EC, the move towards economic and political union were noted but debated largely in the context of money - whether the current EC level of direct aid would continue, how the Common Agricultural Policy would be affected, whether the economy could withstand the scrapping of the trade barriers. The social implications of the changes were barely discussed.

In 1990, as in the previous three years since Fianna Fáil had come to power on a mandate to sort out Ireland's financial miasma, political debate focussed almost exclusively on the state of the economy, with some sideline interest in northern Ireland matters, most notably Ireland's contentious extradition arrangements with the United Kingdom.

There was a tendency among some of the more careless elements of the business community to refer to the country as Ireland Inc, testimony to the increasing narrowness of focus on the kind of society Ireland was becoming. Social policy debate, when it took place at all, focussed on poverty and unemployment, the growing AIDS problem, housing and homelessness.

Most definitely off the political agenda were the twin bogeys of abortion and divorce. Public and politicians alike had little stomach for the reactivation of these issues following the hugely divisive, draining, referenda of 1983 and 1986 in which the forces of the country's small liberal alliance had been roundly beaten off the battle field - at least for the foreseeable future.

The Pro-Life Amendment Campaign of 1983 which resulted

in a constitutional ban on abortion had also brought to the surface a powerful Catholic conservative elite who would dominate and control the social legislation agenda for the rest of the decade. By 1990, they were widely seen as invincible.

These people, among them the cream of the Irish professional classes, barristers, lecturers, doctors, business people and clergy, were highly articulate, motivated, well-funded Catholic ideologues embedded in a host of organisations and front organisations around the country. Their contacts reached the highest levels of Government. Their most public face, Family Solidarity, had a membership network which reached into every Catholic parish in Ireland.

The 1983 Constitutional Amendment was reinforced in 1986 by a further referendum when the Irish people voted to retain the constitutional ban on divorce.

By the late 1980s the liberal agenda had been trampled into the ground. Activists slunk off to lick their wounds. Former supporters in the political parties no longer wished to know.

The fall-out from the 'Pro-Life' victory continued, with a ban on the dissemination of abortion information and an effective prohibition on imported magazines such as *Cosmopolitan*, which carried advertisements for abortion clinics in their classified sections. University students were brought to court charged with providing abortion information in their campus literature.

A European Court of Human Rights ruling, secured by Senator Mary Robinson, declaring that Irish laws on homosexuality were in breach of the Human Rights Convention was left to gather dust back home, the ruling Fianna Fáil/Progressive Democrat (PD) coalition fearing a conservative backlash if they moved to act on the Court's finding.

A widely distributed Family Solidarity booklet on homosexuality depicted male homosexuals as amoral disease carriers, the timing of the publication, in the wake of the European Court ruling clearly designed to stifle any Government enforcement initiative.

Lip service continued to be paid to the problems of marital breakdown, to the continuing stream of women travelling across the Irish Sea to the abortion clinics of Liverpool and London, but there was little or no political will to actually do anything to alleviate the confusion and hardship, and the once active pro-choice and pro-divorce lobbies were now dormant.

In effect, the country's elected legislators had surrendered to an unelected, external force, the shadowy, powerful men and women behind Family Solidarity, SPUC, and other such bodies. Twice the legislators had been bitten by this extra-parliamentary force and no one was about to put their hands out to be bloodied a third time.

So they sat on them instead.

By 1990, on a party political level, it was increasingly evident that several of the major Dáil parties were experiencing crises of identity. Some knew this, others didn't.

Fianna Fáil was one of those that didn't. The country's largest party, it had been forced to go into coalition with the Progressive Democrats after the 1989 General Election, a decision that had traumatised the party's rank and file.

Over the years Fianna Fáil had gradually watered down its adherence to the party's founding aims and other so-called 'core values'. It was no longer quite so gung ho in its Republicanism having being forced to toe the line on the 1985 Anglo-Irish Agreement, and on new extradition arrangements with the United Kingdom.

The move to a politically and economically united Europe had also captivated party leader Charles J Haughey despite his party's earlier opposition to the Single European Act, the foundation stone of the new Europe. Haughey, now Taoiseach, would hold the office of EC Council President for the first six months of 1990. And this new Europe which he would enthusiastically promote for those six months had no place for the outdated, narrowly nationalist myths and beliefs to which some in Fianna Fáil still clung and which Haughey and others cynically exploited when it came to election time.

With the crumbling of the old party core values - the revival of the Irish language, the protection of the small rural landowner, economic independence - much of Haughey's difficulty was to find some other set of all-embracing truths that would unite his supporters once again, allowing Fianna Fáil to continue in its role as the country's catch-all, dominant party. If he didn't the party was unlikely ever again to rule alone.

The election of the country's President, on 7 November 1990, would give a public verdict on the state of Fianna Fáil in the new decade.

In line with the new European ethos, which held the party leader so much in thrall, would Fianna Fáil choose to field a candidate who reflected the new political realities, or seek to regain favour with the grassroots by trotting out an old reliable, a politician intimately identified with the fading values of the past?

But in the short term, it was the largest opposition party, Fine Gael, that had the most difficult job in carving out an identity, a *raison d'être*, for itself.

Following the 1987 election which saw a minority Fianna Fáil Government in power with a strong mandate to cut public spending and curb the spiralling debt crisis and budget deficit, Fine Gael had no real political option but to support the Government on its economic plans. The alternative was another General Election which the party could afford neither financially nor politically.

The resulting 'Tallaght Strategy' formalised that support and proved hard to swallow for many Fine Gael supporters. It may have been a commendable move, beneficial to the public interest, but it left the party floundering for a role and identity distinct from that of Fianna Fáil whose economic platform it was now rowing in behind.

Since many of the social policy initiatives which the party had been associated with during the 1980s were now effectively out of bounds it proved increasingly difficult for party leader Alan Dukes to strike significant points of difference between his party and that of Charlie Haughey.

Garret Fitzgerald's leadership of Fine Gael which ended in 1987, had brought the party to within five seats of Fianna Fáil. His so-called 'Constitutional Crusade' which collapsed ignominiously during the referenda had energised the party, boosted its membership and carved out a distinctive niche on the political spectrum. When that failed, when Fianna Fáil adopted much the same economic strategy as Fine Gael, and when the Progressive Democrats emerged on the scene, Fine Gael was left ideologically naked.

The problem worsened with the 1989 General Election. Now in coalition with the PDs, Fianna Fáil no longer needed opposition support. Relieved of the Tallaght Strategy it was now up to Dukes to carve out a clearer political agenda and identity for his party. But as the decade ended, it was increasingly clear that he simply couldn't do it.

Party frustration was vented on the leader. With the Presidential Election looming towards the end of the year Dukes's energies had begun to concentrate not on policy or election strategy, but on survival. For him the election was the ultimate test of his leadership.

In contrast to Fine Gael, the small left-wing Labour Party appeared to be flourishing. The left vote had almost doubled in the 1989 election and Labour leader Dick Spring manouevred to capitalise on his party's gains. Unlike Fine Gael, Labour did have an ideological basis to its opposition to Government economic policy and did not have to pull its punches when it went on the attack. Dick Spring became a formidable Dáil orator, constantly trumping Alan Dukes when it came to spotting Government misdeeds.

When the East European regimes collapsed, and the country's centre and right-wing intelligentsia proceeded to laud the death of socialism, it was the smaller, marxist Workers' Party that took the brunt of the cat-calling leaving Labour largely unscathed.

Time and time again, when Workers' Party leader Proinsías De Rossa stood to criticise the Government on some issue, Haughey would move to silence him by throwing out the latest report of some appalling atrocity committed by one of the former East European regimes.

By 1990 the Workers' Party, despite its success in 1989, was also a party in crisis, with a smouldering internal debate about how should it situate itself on the political spectrum in the wake of the East European collapse.

By 1990 Dick Spring's mind was already moving towards expanding the party's ideological base thereby increasing its support. He also wanted to secure Labour's left-wing dominance in the Dáil. The global mood of anti-socialism lent urgency to his plans.

Alone of the three parties who would field candidates in the Presidential Election, Spring was very clear about what he wanted it to achieve.

*

That was the setting for the 1990 Presidential Election.

The country which had not voted for a President since 1973, (President Patrick Hillery had been an agreed choice in 1976 and again in 1983) would elect its head of state in a situation of great flux on the European and world stage while, on the domestic front, major ideological and other changes were taking place within the political parties.

Unlike a General Election, the Presidential race would confer no executive role on the winner. But precisely because of that, the public could, in its vote, make a statement about Ireland and its future without fear of upsetting the short-term political apple cart. The political parties could also use it for their own ends - sorting out the leadership crisis for Fine Gael; shifting direction and triumphing over the Workers' Party for Labour.

Fianna Fáil did not yet see the election as any sort of turning point for them. But they would.

Much of this analysis is, of course, retrospective, made with hindsight. In January 1990 when the Presidential Election first began to impinge on the public consciousness, no one saw it in those terms.

For Fianna Fáil, it was just another election which they were racing favourites to win. For Fine Gael too, it was just another election and a headache they could well do without at a time of great uncertainty within the party. They would field a candidate who would probably come second.

Dick Spring was the only party leader who actively looked forward to the election. And alone of all the party leaders it was he who would choose a candidate who not only wanted the job but who had a political agenda of her own to pursue should she win.

The presence of Mary Robinson, so closely identified with the most contentious social issues on the political agenda, would bring a new and unexpected dimension to the saga about to unfold. Twice her side had been defeated in its efforts to bring about a more progressive, liberal, pluralist society and now the battle would be joined again.

As one commentator put it: this was round three.

1

Spin the Bottle

Of the three potential Fine Gael nominees, neither Avril Doyle nor Austin Currie measured up to an acceptable level on any criterion. Each received minority support on their suitability as candidates, both in overall terms and among Fine Gael supporters, and neither were seen as likely to represent Ireland well abroad, or to relate well to the people of Ireland. Furthermore, neither is given the remotest chance of being elected.
Confidential Fine Gael research conducted by the Market Research Bureau of Ireland (MRBI)
16 to 30 July, 1990.

It is customary in political parties that whenever market researchers deliver their findings in the privacy of the party's headquarters, no comment is made until after the researchers have left. So, in mid-August 1990, the head of the Market Research Bureau of Ireland, Jack Jones, delivered his executive commentary on the company's July survey of the electorate's attitude to the forthcoming Presidential Election to an impassive Fine Gael leader Alan Dukes and an equally impassive General Secretary Joe Kenny.

What they heard would have made stronger men weep. The man that Dukes was now actively chasing as party presidential candidate - worse, the only one he had the remotest chance of securing - was, according to Mr Jones, for the purposes of this election a dud. Austin Currie, the former SDLP politician, a TD in the constituency of Dublin West for little over a year, held no attraction for the wider electorate.

Currie had had an illustrious career in northern politics, prominent in the early Civil Rights movement, later becoming a Stormont Minister. But with the imposition of direct rule, and the shelving of the Stormont Assembly in the mid-1980s, he had become largely politically redundant. What saved him was a call from former Fine Gael leader Garret Fitzgerald and an invitation to stand for the party in the 1989 General Election, in Dublin West.

Mr Jones folded away his charts. Mr Dukes thanked him, complimented him on the quality of his work and showed him the door.

The two men were shattered by the survey, commissioned by Kenny and Dukes without any apparent consultation with the party front bench. For them, the Presidential Election was not a matter of 'visions', 'new dawns', or the setting of new political agendae. It was a simple matter of the leader's survival. Every stomach-turning statistic about Currie in the survey was one more nail in Dukes's political coffin.

The relationship between Kenny and Dukes was quite extraordinary. They were each other's best friend and confidante, in a relationship which had come to exclude virtually every other Fine Gael activist and Oireachtas member. Individual front benchers believed that other front benchers were on Dukes's inside track but over time such relationships had been whittled away until, in the end, only Joe was left.

Political colleagues found Dukes intensely difficult to relate to. There was failure to empathise, to click on an emotional level. But in the ebullient, friendly, intensely likeable 'cute hoor operator' Joe Kenny, the party leader had found a soul mate. And it was a relationship that enraged his front bench - in their eyes, Kenny was Dukes's 'agent'.

By the summer of 1990 Dukes was actively loathed by a significant number of his front and back benchers. By the time the party's presidential campaign began in September he could count among his front bench loyalists only Alan Shatter, Gay Mitchell, Madeleine Taylor-Quinn, Dinny McGinley, Jim O'Keeffe, and Ted Nealon. By the time the campaign ended, even fewer would raise even a whisper in support.

There was a simple reason for Mr Dukes's problems. As party leader he simply couldn't hack it - he lacked big-time political *nous* and local councillors showed more savvy in dealing with their political colleagues than did Dukes. For a man with perfect leadership credentials, on paper, he was a bumbling neophyte when it came to cutting it on the floor of the Dáil.

Time and time again, Labour leader Dick Spring had triumphed over Alan Dukes in virtuoso performances on issue after issue, leading commentators to dub the super-slick Mr Spring as the real leader of the opposition. Much of Spring's headline-hogging stunts had more to do with style than with substance, a fact which greatly frustrated Mr Dukes.

Dukes had never accepted the role of table-thumping rhetoric in Dáil politics. For him reason reigned supreme. "I am pure reason," he boasted once to a colleague, not grasping that his party wanted, needed, the odd, irrational, table-thumping, morale-boosting rant as well.

By the summer it was open season on Dukes in the press with endless comparisons between him and the Labour leader and increasing hints about disaffection in the ranks.

Spring's most effective performance would come later that August, during the emergency Dáil debate to push through emergency legislation to bail out the Taoiseach and Fianna Fáil leader Charles J Haughey's one-time crony Larry Goodman, and the beef industry of which Mr Goodman controlled an unfortunately high percentage.

Even worse than the brilliance of Spring's oratory was the revelation that bankers, with crucial information about Goodman, had chosen to leak information, not to their philosophical soul mates, Fine Gael, but to the socialist (at least as they were then) Labour Party.

For his front bench enemies it was another stick with which to beat the 'Ceannaire', the sneering title used by former Fine Gael TD John Boland in his vitriolic attacks on the leader in *The Sunday Business Post*. Although it was never stated explicitly, it underpinned the entire Fine Gael election campaign - if Dukes failed to return from the electoral outing with more than 25% he could pack his bags.

*

But back in the spring of 1990 only desultory attention was being paid to the upcoming Presidential Election. It was, for a start, an office that few could summon much enthusiasm for - an office distant from the people either won or granted by Fianna Fáil since the foundation of the State and which served a function few could understand or articulate.

Remembered images of Dr Patrick Hillery's fourteen years in

office were of a nice man in a cape inspecting endless guards of
honour; sedate footage of black-tie dinners with obscure heads of
state; or of Hillery facing the gales in his beloved County Clare.
Golf figured prominently in what people most remembered the
President doing. Much of the energy of all three campaigns
would go on devising a previously unimagined role for the
President, free of honour guards and airport steps.

If there was talk, it centred around the local elections.
Divisions had emerged between the coalition partners about
when the elections should be held and opposition parties were
trying to second-guess their deliberations.

Fianna Fáil, organisationally in disarray since the 1989
coalition deal with the Progressive Democrats, needed the
elections like a hole in the head. The PDs however were rearing
to go, anxious to put in place a local councillor network in
preparation for the next General Election.

Fine Gael reasoned that the local elections would probably be
held on the same day as the presidential one, to save money. It
was talk of that kind that slowly began to focus minds on the
issue.

At that stage, most Fine Gael people would have assumed
that Garret Fitzgerald would be their candidate, if the election
was to be contested. He had the kind of broad appeal that could
win votes beyond the party's normal support base. But as early as
Christmas 1989 Fitzgerald had indicated privately that he had no
intention of contesting the Presidency. Dáil politics, he said, was
all about policies, which he loved, and kissing babies, which he
did not. And the Presidency was all about kissing babies.

Meanwhile the party Ard Fheis was looming. Almost as an
afterthought, Dukes decided to make some reference to the
Presidency to give party members something to look forward to.

His own belief was that Fitzgerald might not run, but that the
party's former deputy leader and now Foreign Affairs
spokesperson, Peter Barry, almost certainly would. He knew
there was going to be a contest, the Labour Party had already
announced they would be fielding a candidate and Fianna Fáil
would almost certainly nominate the Minister for Defence and
Tánaiste, Brian Lenihan.

But as soon as he uttered the now infamous phrase, on the
podium of Dublin's Point Depot, that he would produce "a

candidate of vigour and stature," Dukes knew he had made a big mistake. Not only did those gathered in the hall immediately conclude that he was referring to Fitzgerald, they also leapt to their feet and cheered.

Fitzgerald's stricken, embarrassed face told Dukes all he needed to know. Hell would freeze over before Garret ran. Worse, he had now raised expectations among the grassroots who had demonstrated very clearly that they wanted Fitzgerald and no one else.

*

And so the chase began - Dukes's and Kenny's desperate five month search for a candidate, any candidate, a farcical trawling exercise described by one party member as like a "bizarre game of spin the bottle."

Some time after the Ard Fheis a list of potential candidates was drawn up at a series of front bench meetings and individual TDs were delegated specific people to approach. Many on the list were political has-beens, prominent figures of the 1970s and early 1980s whom the public had long since forgotten. At this stage no research had been done to guide them as to what the voters wanted in a candidate and no one within the party had a vision of anyone other than a faithful old party retainer with no skeletons in the cupboard. There was no discussion as to what the Presidency was about or what a future Fine Gael President could achieve. The emphasis was simply on finding a candidate and preferably one who fitted as near as dammit the image that Hillery had presented. Though perhaps with a bit more pep.

The late coalition Minister and Attorney General John Kelly, a potentially excellent candidate, given the man's style, wit and ability to attract more than the party's core vote, was approached by Fine Gael deputy leader John Bruton. Kelly by now had dropped out of mainstream politics having declined to contest the General Election in 1989. He thanked Bruton politely for the honour and said no thanks.

MEP and former coalition Minister Paddy Cooney, another old party stalwart, was also approached around the early summer. He too declined the honour, as did Mark Clinton (former Minister for Agriculture) when Alan Dukes sounded him out.

High Court Judge Declan Costello, author of the party's famous *Just Society* document in the 1960's was approached by Garret Fitzgerald but he too declined the offer as he had ceased all political involvement when he was appointed to the Bench.

Then Dukes tried Tom O'Donnell, a former Fine Gael Minister and MEP, a man firmly on the party right wing who, along with his sister Bernadette Bonar, had been a significant mover in the Pro-Life Amendment campaign in 1983 and the anti-divorce campaign in 1986. The news that Dukes had actually approached O'Donnell horrified even his closest colleagues. The man's appeal would scarcely stretch to the core vote let alone go beyond it. And how could Dukes justify putting forward a man so radically opposed to the leader's own liberal values?

Dukes then proposed to approach Tom Raftery, a former party MEP. Few people felt the idea had any merit, given Raftery's low profile and lack of broad political experience. In the end, the increasingly desperate leader was dissuaded from his plan by Joe Kenny.

By now the media was getting great value out of the candidate saga, with names popping up every other week in the news pages. In some cases the names were deliberately leaked by party members desperate to get them shot down before the idea of actually selecting some of the wackier ones took hold. At one extraordinary meeting of a group of activists, the idea of putting forward some anonymous 'ordinary person in the street' was actively considered.

Despite later denials, Dukes also floated the name of Kerry playwright John B Keane. It was not Dukes who suggested to Kerry TD Jimmy Deenihan that he should approach him, but he did mention the name to at least one member of the front bench. Deenihan himself was approached by a number of TDs, including Austin Deasy, to sound Keane out. So he did, asking him casually across the bar in Keane's Listowel pub one night what he thought of the idea. Keane told him that he didn't think much of it. While Keane, a hugely likeable and popular man, may well have been a good candidate, the leaked news that he'd been approached suggested certain difficulties in the party's selection process, to put it mildly.

Dukes, embarrassed by the continuous media speculation, then asked his colleagues to simply slip him lists of possible names rather than run the risk of having them leaked by discussing them at party meetings. Other names considered included Garret Fitzgerald's former adviser Jim Dooge, Senator Avril Doyle, former TD and European Commissioner Richard Burke, another former Commissioner Peter Sutherland and Fine Gael MEP Mary Banotti. John Boland's later claim that Austin Currie was the party's seventeenth choice wasn't too far off the mark.

*

In early summer Austin Currie's name was mooted at a front bench meeting. According to one frontbencher, the name was greeted "with a guffaw". They felt that Currie, new to southern politics, was simply not a credible choice.

In fact Currie's name had been floating around the outer margins of the party for quite some time. He had first been suggested to Dukes in the spring by Garret Fitzgerald, the man responsible for introducing Currie to southern politics.

But, with the suggestion apparently rejected by the front bench, the idea of selecting a former Minister of more recent vintage than Paddy Cooney or Richard Burke emerged. Days later Dublin West TD, and spokesperson on Communications, Jim Mitchell was invited for a private chat with Alan Dukes.

Mitchell, an excellent operator in constituency elections, thought that Dukes was about to invite him to be the campaign Director of Elections, a prospect that sent shivers down his spine.

By this stage Mitchell had written off Dukes. The final straw had been a major row between the two men during the passage of the controversial Broadcasting Bill in April 1990.

Mitchell had scooped the other opposition parties by discovering that the Government planned to help out the new so-called independent radio stations by siphoning off advertising and licence revenue from RTE. Then, to Mitchell's intense humiliation and anger he discovered that Dukes had had a private meeting with the Taoiseach to discuss the future of the independent national radio station, Century. Only pressure from his colleagues persuaded Mitchell not to resign but he lashed

Dukes privately and had still not forgiven him for going behind his back, interfering in his own policy area.

In his office Dukes greeted his frontbencher in an extravagantly friendly way, ushering him across the room to sit on the casual chairs, side by side. The party leader then told him how terrific, he, Mitchell was, how he exuded *gravitas* and good humour, how popular he was, finishing with the exhortation "You must run for President!"

Mitchell simply burst out laughing. Then he stopped, not wishing to appear bad-mannered. Then, to close off any further embarrassing discussion and exit the room fast, he told Dukes he'd think about it and scuttled off down the corridor.

Mitchell did give the suggestion some thought. He talked to colleagues about it, some of whom urged him to run, most forcefully Madeleine Taylor-Quinn. A week later, however, he rang Joe Kenny asking him to tell Dukes (who was in Europe at the time) that the answer "to the other thing" was "no".

The situation was now at crisis point. Mary Robinson had been nominated on May Day by the Labour Party. While Fianna Fáil would not formally select their candidate until the autumn of 1990, it was a racing certainty that Brian Lenihan would be their choice.

Desperate measures were needed. Jim Mitchell had suggested setting up a high-level commission to sort out the whole mess but the idea was never accepted by Dukes. Then Joe Kenny suggested a *council of war* type meeting to which Dukes would invite Garret Fitzgerald and Peter Barry, and other influential party members to flush them out once and for all, and put pressure on the two men to run.

Dukes agreed, but opted to hold the meeting at a private dinner at the Grey Door restaurant. Kenny instinctively felt that this was a bad idea - the atmosphere would be far too social and congenial, the lads would settle down to discuss old war stories and nothing would be achieved.

And he was absolutely right.

The dinner was very hush-hush, attended by Fitzgerald, Barry, Dukes, Mitchell, Finance spokesperson Michael Noonan, former EC Commissioner Peter Sutherland and Peter Shanley SC, later to become Deputy Director of Elections. The entire evening was a disaster. Neither Barry or Fitzgerald were prepared to budge an inch from their stated positions. When Peter Sutherland attempted to put moral pressure on Barry by telling him that the party needed him to run, Barry replied that in that case he should run himself. Kenny's plan that the meeting would also form the basis for an election strategy committee and come up with a fund raising agenda also got nowhere. These ideas were simply never discussed. When Dukes met Kenny the following day he told him that it had seemed "like a good idea at the time."

Dukes and Mitchell then began pursuing two different agendae. Shortly after the Grey Door dinner, with no option left, the party leader had decided to make a play for Austin Currie.

His name now began to be mentioned in the corridors of Leinster House and Currie soon realised that he was being actively, if covertly, head-hunted. People began approaching him in the bar to discuss the Presidency. Currie assumed they were being put up to it in some way but simply laughed when asked directly if he'd be interested and told them no.

Then on 19 July Alan Dukes phoned Currie and asked to make an appointment to meet him. He said he wanted to discuss the state of his political mind. Currie replied that he and his wife Annita were going on a fortnight's holiday to Yugoslavia the following day but would meet him when he returned. He was pretty sure he knew exactly what was on Dukes's mind.

To Currie's surprise Dukes later tracked down his hotel in Yugoslavia and rang to firm up a date for the meeting. This was arranged for 5 August. Annita and Austin would travel down to the Dukes home in Kildare and stay overnight.

*

Meanwhile Jim Mitchell, unaware of the approach to Currie, had decided to go hell for leather and attempt to get Peter Barry to run. Every July the Mitchell family decamped to Schull in County Cork for their annual sailing holiday. Peter Barry wasn't too far away. He and his family owned a holiday home in Ballylickey, just fifteen miles from Schull. The Barrys and the Mitchells often met up during July, occasionally joined by Fine Gael TDs Jim O'Keeffe and Garret Fitzgerald who also holidayed in West Cork.

Arriving in Schull in early July, Mitchell telephoned Barry's secretary in Cork to enquire when Peter was due in Ballylickey. She told him he was due down later that evening. "Here's our chance," Mitchell told his wife Patsy, and the two drove off to Ballylickey. They knew that Margaret Barry, Peter's wife, would be there. They planned to put pressure on her, in Barry's absence, to get him to run.

The Mitchells arrived in time for afternoon tea. The three were old friends but Margaret politely brushed aside their entreaties. Their family, their friends, all were in Cork; the Presidency would take them away from that. There was no question of her putting pressure on Peter to run. In addition, Barry too was disenchanted with Dukes, reluctant to do anything to bail his leader out.

But still Mitchell persisted. A few days later a dinner was arranged for the Journey's End restaurant in Crookhaven. In attendance were the Mitchells, the Barrys, Frank Boland, former chairperson of Aer Rianta and Judy Boland, Irish Sugar Company chairperson Bernie Cahill and Kathleen Cahill, the Managing Director of Saab in Ireland, Gabby Hogan (a good friend of Garret Fitzgerald) and Jacintha Hogan.

It was a high-powered gathering and all were there, at Mitchell's insistence and as much for the crack as for the more urgent item on Mitchell's agenda, to get Barry to run. All tried. All failed. The following day Mitchell rang Dukes to say that Barry was a hopeless case - there was no way he was going to run.

Then, at the beginning of August, just a few days before Currie was due to return from Yugoslavia, Mitchell returned briefly to his Dublin office. While there, his brother Gay, a Dukes supporter, rang to say that he had returned from his family holiday in Connemara and wanted to meet him.

Later that evening Gay arrived out at Mitchell's Terenure home. He told him that he and Wexford TD Ivan Yates had been to see Dukes and that he had sent them out to Jim to persuade him to run. He then reiterated the same line Dukes had used on Mitchell several months earlier - that he had *gravitas*, good humour, was popular and so on and so forth. An inconclusive discussion continued in a local pub. The following week, about four days after Currie was due to meet with Dukes, Gay Mitchell contacted his brother again in Dublin. Forget the whole thing, he said, it's Currie he's after now ...

The search had now descended into sheer farce, with Barry, Mitchell and Currie being head-hunted simultaneously, Dukes hedging his bets on all three and Jim Mitchell in the peculiar position of being both head and hunter.

Currie, in Yugoslavia, was unaware of the attempts still being made to inveigle other people into the Presidential net. Returning to Dublin on 4 August, he and Annita arrived in Kildare the next day, Sunday, shortly before dinner.

Dukes broached the subject immediately. He told him he was sure he had a pretty good idea of what he wanted to talk about. Currie said he did and that he wasn't interested. He told Dukes that he was too young (at the age of fifty) and that neither his activists nor his constituents in Dublin West could tolerate being disrupted again by Fine Gael. Former EC Commissioner Richard Burke had resigned his seat in the constituency in controversial circumstances, and the TD who succeeded him, Liam Skelly, had also caused headaches for the party. Party activists were fed up. For their sakes he simply couldn't run. He had given them certain commitments when he was elected, he added, and didn't want to go back on his word. Currie also felt, correctly, that his short period in southern Irish politics would be held against him and that people would wonder who the hell he thought he was.

But Currie had other, private, reasons for not running, reasons he kept to himself that night. He knew that the presidential campaign could not be divorced from the leadership issue. If he ran he would need the united support of TDs who might judge his candidacy or the degree to which they should stir themselves in the campaign in proportion to their feelings about Dukes. Currie did not want to be a sacrificial lamb in an internal feud. He had not been in the party long enough to build up his own network of TD support and felt he would be extremely vulnerable to party apathy.

So that night Currie said no. The matter was discussed some more later on with Dukes admitting that Garret Fitzgerald was the preferred choice but that he was still hopeful that Peter Barry might run. The Curries left the following day still saying no but feeling that Dukes would continue to keep up the pressure. It was obvious to Austin Currie at that stage that Dukes would have done anything to get a candidate.

Two weeks later, on 16 August, Mitchell was again up in Dublin. Millionaire businessman Michael Smurfit had called him to say that Brigitta Smurfit was coming to town, and invited the Mitchells to dinner. So back Mitchell went to Schull to collect Patsy where he was contacted by Alan Dukes seeking a meeting back in Dublin the following day.

Mitchell arrived in Dublin with just an hour to spare before the Smurfit dinner. The MRBI research had just been received by the party leader. Dukes told Mitchell that it was clear that Currie should be the last person to run and that Peter Barry had emerged again as the obvious candidate. He wanted Mitchell to do everything he could to persuade Barry and to get people in to help. Mitchell told him that he'd already done everything he could to cajole Barry, but would sound out the situation once again.

The MRBI research was certainly damning.

Six people were rated for suitability for the office of President on several different criteria: Brian Lenihan; Mary Robinson; Peter Barry; Marine Minister John Wilson; Avril Doyle and Austin Currie.

Austin Currie definitely came last, with Lenihan first, followed by Robinson, Barry, Wilson, and Doyle. The scores for the candidates were:

Brian Lenihan	3.91
Mary Robinson	3.70
Peter Barry	3.54
John Wilson	2.94
Avril Doyle	2.86
Austin Currie	2.74

According to the five point scale of suitability, MRBI told Fine Gael that anything below 3.5 was unsatisfactory, a candidate on that rating had no hope of being elected, so neither Avril Doyle nor Austin Currie measured up to an acceptable level on any criterion. "Neither is given the remotest chance of being likely to be elected, if nominated."

Other MRBI findings showed why Dukes was now even more anxious than ever to persuade Peter Barry. The report stated:

The current impact of Peter Barry indicates some degree
of potential, and of the six personalities, he is positioned
in third place, marginally behind the already nominated
Mary Robinson, on almost all criteria. At this stage he is
rated equal to her on basic suitability, on representing
Ireland well abroad, and on relating well to people. He is
positioned in second place to Brian Lenihan on being
well known, which is, however, not classified as a very
important criterion. Peter Barry is seen as suitable by
three in every four Fine Gael supporters and by a
marginal majority of those in Fianna Fáil.

Seventy five per cent of Fine Gael voters considered Peter
Barry either very suitable or reasonably suitable for office,
compared with just 37% who saw Currie as suitable. More
disturbingly, 66% of Fine Gael voters, almost twice as many,
saw Mary Robinson as suitable for office, and 63% saw Lenihan
as suitable.

Fifteen per cent of Fine Gael voters stated they would not like
Currie as President compared with 12% who said they wouldn't
like Lenihan to be elected. Only 3% said no to Peter Barry.

And the reason for the anti-Currie feeling? That was
contained in the last question of the survey. Asked why they
would not like to see certain candidates elected, a staggering
70% of those who said they would not vote for him said,
unprompted, that it was because of his northern background.

The survey also disclosed why Mary Robinson could pose a
serious threat to Fine Gael's chances of winning, already hinting
at what was to become the major issue of the campaign. The
report stated:

Mary Robinson has, at this stage, created a strong
impact; she is second to Brian Lenihan on suitability,
and equal to Peter Barry on representing Ireland and
relating to the people, and is ahead of all other
candidates on her likelihood of remaining independent
of the Government of the day - which is seen as an
important criterion.

In addition, Robinson and Lenihan were the only two
candidates who majorities in *all* parties saw as a suitable
candidate for the Presidency.

That weekend Mitchell travelled to Galway to collect his children from relatives, before heading back to Schull for the final weeks of the summer break. In Galway he put through repeated calls to Barry's home in Cork city and his holiday home in Ballylickey. He had forgotten that Barry was attending the Michael Collins commemoration that weekend at Béal na mBláth, where he would come under further pressure from Cork activists in a move overseen by Joe Kenny in Fine Gael headquarters.

En route to Schull, Mitchell stayed overnight at the holiday home of Michael Noonan in Foynes. On Sunday morning the two men again attempted to contact Barry. Neither phone was answered. Finally, on Sunday afternoon Margaret Barry answered and told the two men that Peter was at the Collins ceremonies. "I know what you're about," she added, "and you can forget it."

Just then Peter Barry arrived back. Both Mitchell and Noonan spoke to him telling him of the damning research findings. Barry remained resolute. I will not run, he told them, tell Dukes to forget it.

The following week, on 28 and 29 August the Dáil was reconvened for the Goodman emergency debate.

There was now a palpable feeling of crisis among Fine Gael TDs and Senators, with hushed discussions and hurried meetings in corridors and private rooms. The feeling was widespread that Dukes would not find a candidate and would be toppled as a consequence. For many in the party, and particularly in the front bench, this was the most appetising option. Currie was still adamantly refusing to run.

"It was felt that Currie was right," said one frontbencher, "that he'd be mad to run and that it would be better for the party if he didn't, better from the point of view that we were going to be humiliated in the election anyway and also from the point of view that the leader thing, if he ran, would only be deferred. The leadership would have to be addressed. A new leader would have been free to say, look, I've made no commitments about candidates, I'm going to go in behind Mary Robinson. There would have been no big deal about it. But that wasn't to be."

Dukes knew only too well the plot that was unfolding. On 28 August he again called Currie into his office and asked him to run. Again Currie refused. Dukes called him back again the following day and again Currie said no.

By now the word was out that Currie was still being actively pursued and those still loyal to Dukes put enormous pressure on him to accept the nomination. It had been a mistake for Currie to return to the Dáil. He was a sitting duck for pressure. On Wednesday 29 August, he gave an interview to a reporter from *The Dublin Tribune* stating categorically that he would not run.

The pressure mounted. He was told that the party needed a candidate, that it would be intolerable if they didn't find one, that he wouldn't do himself any harm by running, that the party was low in the polls and that a good campaign would increase its standing. Nobody suggested that he would finish third. None but the few who had seen the research could have imagined it.

On Thursday Currie fled. He did his weekly advice clinic in Blanchardstown but instead of spending the night as he normally did, in his Lucan base, he headed north to his Dungannon home, away from all pressure.

The same day both Noonan and Mitchell were called in by Dukes. Both told him bluntly that the situation was very serious. He had committed the party to a candidate and he now had to find one by the following week, 5 September, the date of the next parliamentary party meeting.

They didn't need to make the threat explicit - should he fail to produce a candidate in six days time, he would be ousted from the party leadership.

The following day Dukes rang Dungannon. Currie, who had never refused point blank to meet Dukes, asked him to suggest a venue. Neither man wanted to meet anywhere in Dublin or Kildare for fear of detection. Dukes eventually said he'd drive up to Tyrone.

That night Dukes arrived at the Glengannon Hotel shortly after 6:00pm. They briefly discussed the situation and then drove back to Currie's home where the matter was thrashed out in front of the family. It was patently clear that Currie was the only option left. Dukes told him straight out that the party was committed to having a candidate and that no one else would do it. It was hardly the most flattering line of argument but it worked ...

Currie explained once again that his strongest reservation was his Dublin West constituency. Dukes said he was prepared to meet and talk with the activists and Currie agreed to set it up. The leader left shortly after midnight to drive back to Dublin.

At this stage Currie was convinced that his constituency activists simply wouldn't wear it but he agreed to go through the motions and spent the weekend contacting them, meeting them back in Dublin on Monday 3 September. He explained the position fully, outlining the pros and cons. They maintained that they still had huge reservations. They didn't want to disrupt the constituency, they didn't want Currie to be damaged and some of them also had reservations about Dukes. Those present included councillor Jim Fay, Lucan auctioneer Gerry Leahy, Corduff teacher John Lynch, originally from the north, former constituency organiser Brian Brady and constituency chairperson Tom Kavanagh.

The activists told Currie that he had a great future in the party and that getting involved in something so intimately linked with the leadership battle would harm him. The meeting ended with the activists still resolutely opposed to his running and Currie telling them that he would not run without their support.

Earlier that day Currie had also told Senator Maurice Manning that he would not be running. Manning told him that he had made the right decision.

The following day, Tuesday, just forty-eight hours before the deadline parliamentary party meeting, Currie met Dukes at 11:00am. He told him the outcome of the meeting but Dukes insisted on meeting the team. Currie gave him contact numbers and promised that he would not do anything prior to the meeting to dissuade them from turning up.

Later that evening the meeting took place between the constituency activists, Dukes and Kenny. It lasted almost four hours, with Brian Brady, who would later become Currie's personal assistant on the campaign, being the hardest to budge. Dukes wore them down by insisting over and over again that Currie's position would be enhanced, not damaged by the campaign. The clear implication was that Currie would get a front bench position if he lost. Eventually the men agreed.

Meanwhile, Currie was in bed in Lucan, incapable of sleep. He expected a phone call but none came through. The activists were so stunned by their own *volte face* that they couldn't face him that night. Instead it was Alan Dukes who rang shortly after midnight. He said it was alright, that the men had agreed to support his candidacy. Currie, incredulous, replied that he'd wait to hear it from their own mouths first.

Shortly after 9:00am on Wednesday, just two hours before the front bench meeting, the phone rang. The activist who phoned said they had agreed to support him for the sake of the party and they believed they could sell it to the people of Dublin West.

At 10:00am Currie arrived into Leinster House. In Dukes's office he told him finally that he would agree to stand. Dukes's reply was short. "You have made me," he said, "a very happy man."

The two men then left for the meeting where, according to one frontbencher, the newly resurrected leader "with relief, triumph, and glee," told the meeting that Fine Gael now had a candidate.

So why did Currie run? He had eventually been shown the research - Dukes had volunteered it suggesting that while it looked bad, it only reflected people's opinion on one particular day.

"Currie took a calculated gamble," said one frontbencher. "He had been (involved in politics in the north) for twenty odd years, most of the time his skills under-utilised because of the situation there. And then after years of dejection and depression you're invited to run for Fine Gael in the Dublin West constituency. You take the gamble, you do it, and you get elected. Next thing, a year later, someone asks you to go for President. It's a bit of a dream situation. Now he knows the poll (research findings) and he knows he's going to do badly, but he also gambles that this will enhance his own personal situation, will make him a sort of party favourite, give him a much higher profile and will help him constituency-wise. It's something that he'll dine off for the rest of his life. He'd be invited to all the best diplomatic parties and this, that and the other and so that's why he took the decision he took. He wouldn't lose too much, in fact he'd probably gain and he did by getting a position on the front bench."

That, of course, was the biggest carrot. Alan Dukes never directly offered Currie a place on the front bench if he ran but it was implicit in all their conversations. After the election, when

Dukes was ousted, the one thing he asked incoming leader John Bruton to do was put Currie on his front bench. And he did.

*

And so the scene was set for the most disastrous Fine Gael electoral outing since its foundation, the party saddled with a leader who was at best tolerated, at worst despised by his senior colleagues, who wanted nothing from the election but the retention of his own position; a General Secretary so close to the leadership that his main election agenda was also to keep Dukes's leadership afloat; a mutinous front bench torn between working to give Currie a good show and getting rid of Dukes; sullen back benchers willing to knife themselves if they could knife Dukes as well; the party coffers empty, and a reluctant candidate who they knew had no chance of coming second, let alone winning.

And worst of all, already striding confidently around the country was a candidate, the dark horse Mary Robinson, who Fine Gael supporters cared more for than they ever would for their own 'blow in' from the north ...

2

A Whole Country to Win

If there's one thing that freaks the middle classes more than being found with flying ducks on their wall, it's the fear that they're being manipulated.
Eoghan Harris. (Interview with author January 1991)

There was nothing inevitable about the Robinson victory, nothing determined, and least of all her selection as Labour Party nominee.

Mary Robinson, born Mary Bourke in the western seaboard town of Ballina, County Mayo in 1944, was an unlikely socialist and feminist. Both her parents, Aubrey and the late Tessa (nee O'Donnell), were doctors, well-to-do professionals who afforded their children a superior education coupled with a strong sense of *noblesse oblige*. The supreme confidence in self which Mary Bourke would exhibit throughout her career came both from her education and her family's place in the social order.

The Bourkes were the gentry, the people in the big house who hunted and threw parties that drew the well-to-do of Mayo and beyond, and enticed the farmers and labourers to come and peek as the music and the lights cast a rare glow on the bleak, impoverished Mayo countryside.

Her schooling was private, a local school in Mayo and later in the Sacred Heart Convent of Mount Anville in Dublin where the daughters of the middle classes had their intellects stretched by nuns who displayed more than usual educational vision.

Finishing school was in Paris where a former classmate remembers the academic Ms Bourke, schoolgirl - prim in little fitted suits, and everywhere she went, a fresh pair of snow white gloves.

Mary won a place at Trinity College Dublin (TCD), then open to Catholics only with the permission of the hierarchy. She was a brilliant student, a superb lateral thinker, with great intellectual integrity, capable of arguing at an equal intellectual level with her lecturers.

Then came Harvard, perhaps the single most important defining event in her life. Cast loose in the hotbed of radical thought that was the University in the late sixties, the place of individual personal rights in the enactment of legislation became for her the issue that would underpin all her future work in law and in politics.

Her feminism, her anti-internment stance, her attempts to enact Family Planning legislation, her attitude to the Anglo-Irish Agreement, all came from one simple principle: that personal freedom and the rights of the individual were primary and sacrosanct. It could be argued that, in the strictest sense, she was never a feminist, never a socialist, all the 'isms' were vehicles for advancing her beliefs about the rights of the citizen.

In 1969, now a respected barrister and a law professor at Trinity at the age of twenty-five, she became the first Catholic Senator from Trinity. By 1971 she had introduced a Family Planning bill to the house, the first ever attempt to legalise the import and sale of contraceptives in Ireland.

In 1976 she joined the Labour Party and in 1977 she was imposed on the Rathmines constituency as a candidate in that year's election, attracting just a few hundred votes. In 1981 she ran in Dublin West, trailing in in ninth place behind the Republican H Block candidate.

Her relationship with the Labour Party has been described as 'uneasy'. She lacked empathy with the more working class, traditional Labour culture and they lacked empathy with her middle class background and cerebral approach to party ideology and political activity.

Throughout the seventies her work on civil rights cases had involved her in the growing women's movement. Activists at the time recall with admiration the young barrister, instructing women many years her senior in points of law. Her legal career was outstanding. She is a member of the International Commission of Jurists, which includes some of the most distinguished human rights lawyers in the world.

Her most significant human rights cases included the 1973 Reynolds case seeking the vote for eighteen year olds; the 1976 de Burca case which challenged the jury system as discriminating against women; the Josie Airey case in which Ireland was found to be in breach of the Convention of Human

Rights for failing to provide civil legal aid; the Johnston case which was fundamental in changing the treatment of non-marital children; the Cotter and McDermott case on the equality of social welfare payments for example; the Norris case which resulted in Irish laws on homosexuality being declared in breach of the European Convention of Human Rights.

In 1983 Labour leader and then Tánaiste Dick Spring's decision to overlook her for the position of Attorney General in favour of his friend and political ally John Rogers, deeply angered Robinson though she has always been at pains to point out that it was her antipathy to the 1985 Anglo-Irish Agreement, drawn up without northern Unionist participation, and not her rebuff by Spring, that caused her to leave the party shortly afterwards.

Since 1985 she had focussed fully on her law work, again with the emphasis on issues of civil rights. At the time the Presidential Election was called she was engaged in a freedom to access of information on abortion case in the European Court of Human Rights.

Dick Spring's decision to approach her to become the Labour candidate for the Presidential Election, emerged from a process within the party of defining the type of candidate who could best both represent the party line, and attract votes outside the normal left constituency which, in General Elections, attracted a bare 15% of votes cast.

Spring also wanted a candidate who could break the mould, the stereotypical presidential candidate of ageing party hacks in search of a retirement job, or of docile younger men willing to do the party's bidding, represent the country, and avoid controversy for seven years or even fourteen.

Robinson's name was first mentioned by Denise Rogers, administrative assistant to Ruarí Quinn, the Labour Party's deputy leader, though it had also been tossed around in lists drawn up by Spring and his party adviser Fergus Finlay. The initial approach was made on 14 February by John Rogers and followed up shortly afterwards by a visit by Dick Spring to Robinson's Ranelagh home.

Fergus Finlay, in his book on the Robinson campaign, *Mary Robinson: A President with a Purpose*, wrote that it took 'several meetings' between Labour leader Dick Spring and Mary

Robinson to resolve the major stumbling block in the negotiations - Spring's insistence that she rejoin the Labour Party.

What Finlay does not mention is that at one stage the talks completely broke down with Spring insisting that he couldn't sell an independent candidate to his colleagues and Robinson insisting with equal force that she would never rejoin the party. An early meeting between the two ended with Robinson bidding Spring farewell and telling him, without rancour, that she wished whatever candidate he did choose the very best.

At that stage Mary Robinson was convinced that Spring would not return. Bride Rosney, Robinson's close friend and confidante and deeply politically aware, thought otherwise. The Labour Party, she assured Robinson, needs you more than you need them.

She was right - three weeks later, in mid-March, Dick Spring telephoned stating that he was prepared to run her on Robinson's terms, to get her through the nominating process as an independent.

By this stage Robinson was excited at the idea of running for President. The adrenalin was pumping. Independent Senator Carmencita Hederman's name had been floated and the mould-breaking idea of a relatively young progressive woman as candidate was publicly accepted as plausible.

Bride Rosney found the prospect of a Robinson candidacy "interesting". Already she was wondering what percentage of the poll Mary Robinson would get. Anything less than 20%, the Labour estimate at the time, would be embarrassing. The idea was already growing in her head that the Robinson reach would have to extend way beyond that of the Left.

Later the campaign would be marked by this inner tension, the struggle by the "Robinson camp" to adhere to the political imperatives and etiquette of being a Labour Party nominee, and the desire to keep the party at arm's length.

Bride Rosney, a school teacher who had met Robinson during the Wood Quay protests in the late 1970s, was a major influence on Robinson throughout the campaign. She was blessed with far more political savvy than her friend and was more aware of the need to moderate the Robinson left-liberal image so as to draw in support from constituencies Mary Robinson had never dabbled in before.

Rosney would also become a focus of tension for the Labour Party. Throughout the campaign observers would note a constant tussle for control, even dominance, over Mary Robinson between the party and Rosney.

"Rosney was a brooding, silent, at times anonymous presence throughout the campaign," said one Labour Party activist, "she tended to stir things up, to provoke rows. But there was still a grudging respect (from the party) for a very fine mind. Sometimes I thought she displayed a Svengali complex."

In many ways, the forty-one year old Rosney was the real *éminence grise* of the campaign. A woman largely ignored by the media throughout the election, until Robinson became President and immediately appointed Rosney her personal adviser, she too had rural roots and a background of political, though not party political, activity.

Born in Kerry, the family moved to Dublin when she was still a child. Educated by the Dominican nuns in Eccles Street, Bride Rosney later graduated with a science degree from University College Dublin (UCD). She worked for the Department of Education Curriculum Development Unit, taught in Portmarnock Community School and was eventually appointed principal of Rosmini Community school in Drumcondra, Dublin, a job she held until appointed Robinson's political adviser.

Her remarkable political *nous* was developed through membership of the Teachers' Union of Ireland, An Taisce, and a range of other organisations. Her politics were left of centre, although she never joined the Labour Party. She supported women's rights issues but, during the campaign, told people that she had never been a feminist.

Her friendship with Mary Robinson began in 1978 when Rosney was one of the activists campaigning against the building of civic offices on Dublin's biggest Viking site, and Robinson was Junior Counsel for the protesters in the case taken against them by the building contractor. The friendship became so close that in 1981 Rosney was asked to become godmother to the Robinsons' youngest child, Aubrey.

Many men on the election campaign found it difficult to comprehend or at times cope with the close friendship between the two women. Rosney was not at Robinson's first meeting with

John Rogers when he formally asked her to become a Labour candidate for the nomination, but she was at every meeting Robinson subsequently had with Dick Spring and other politicians and activists.

Those who went to the Robinson home for those early meetings sensed that there was something palpably different about Rosney's place in the scheme of things. She was not just another activist, she was a part of the intimate family circle with an emotional, psychological link to the candidate that no one else could match.

At times she acted almost as a surrogate mother to the Robinson children, William, Tessa and Aubrey. She was the indulgent aunt figure, the keeper of the Kleenex, the buyer of the forbidden ice cream and fizzy drink.

Her loyalty was total. In mediaeval terms, said one observer, she was the Squire to Robinson's Knight willing to do her all when the pair went to battle. On a less altruistic level, others felt that by attaching herself to Robinson, Rosney was in fact implementing her own political agenda. Robinson was someone Rosney herself had chosen to influence, to work through to achieve her own ends.

Robinson's loyalty to Rosney was also total. The rare occasions when she did flare up during the campaign were when some activists dared to question her political mentor. She would not tolerate the slightest hint of criticism.

But that was in the future. First Dick Spring had a major hurdle to cross - getting his own hard left to accept Mary Robinson as party nominee. A number of Labour Party members had already approached Dr Noel Browne with a view to securing his candidacy, a move opposed by Spring who didn't want to see that particular faction getting one over him. Spring felt that Browne would be too undisciplined and too old to undertake the type of campaign he had in mind.

His pre-emptive strike, proposing her name as the Party's candidate, at a meeting of the Parliamentary Party on 4 April, caused uproar. Not at the meeting itself, but later, following the release of a statement saying that he had received the authority of the Parliamentary Party to invite Mary Robinson to stand for selection by the party's Administrative Council. He also telephoned a deeply angry Noel Browne to say that he did not meet the Party's requirements and that he would be putting forward Mary Robinson instead. Spring was effectively presenting the Robinson candidacy as a *fait accompli*, an act which enraged Kildare TD Emmet Stagg who went on air to say that Spring had been given no such authority.

What Stagg and Galway TD Michael D Higgins believed was that Robinson would be just one of the candidates running for the nomination. This was clear in a letter Higgins circulated to members of the Labour Party ten days later.

Stating that he would be proposing Dr Browne as the party candidate at the Administrative Council meeting Higgins added:

> There has been some needless confusion created following reports of the meeting of our Parliamentary Party on Wednesday, 4 April which it is appropriate to dispel. The Party leader announced that he would be putting forward the name of Mary Robinson, a candidate that enjoys the respect and admiration of so many in this country. As we had no agenda item listed, no vote was taken. The general and clear situation was that the Party would now have two excellent candidates from which to make their choice at the joint Administrative Council / Parliamentary Party meeting that, under our Constitution, would follow. There was also the very mature view expressed that whatever candidate was chosen should have the benefit of a totally united and energetic campaign.

Higgins added that he felt that Browne however was "the outstanding candidate" and that the AC (Administrative Council) meeting was "*not* a meeting to *ratify* any previous decision."

Dick Spring clearly didn't agree that this was the case. On 4 April, in a move clearly designed to present not only his own party and Dr Noel Browne with a *fait accompli* but also the Workers' Party, he faxed a message to Workers' Party leader Proinsías De Rossa in Strasbourg inviting talks on the Robinson candidacy but stating: "Please note that the matter will be *formalised* (author's italics) at a joint meeting of our AC/PLP [Administrative Council / Parliamentary Labour Party] at the end of the month."

In the end, Spring weathered the storm. Robinson was

overwhelmingly endorsed and all formerly recalcitrant TDs rowed in behind him to give her their unanimous backing.

But the saga had left a sour taste in Robinson's mouth, angry at being presented as the Labour nominee by Spring before he had properly cleared it with his party.

"It was a total cock up," a member of the 'Robinson camp' within the campaign team said later. "Mary was furious. One of the reasons she had split from the Labour Party over the Anglo-Irish Agreement was because Spring had announced that the Agreement had the unanimous support of the Parliamentary Labour Party. Now here was the same story all over again. She felt that Michael D Higgins and Emmet Stagg, in voicing objections about what Spring had done, were acting honourably but that the whole thing had been handled badly and she told Spring about this in no uncertain terms."

The 4 April announcement of Robinson's nomination for the candidacy by Spring in itself had received little coverage - media interest focussing instead on the row. Robinson's public image was so lacklustre that the *Irish Independent* lumped the story into a small, catch-all news item headed 'Women in Park Race' noting both her potential candidacy and that of Carmencita Hederman.

There was little hint of future greatness, new dawns, or of the intuitive brilliance of Dick Spring.

"On the morning of the fifth of April," says Eoghan Harris, then an RTE producer and who had just left the Workers' Party after a major internal row, "when I opened the papers, what everyone has to keep on remembering, is that there was nothing inevitable. What we had and were given was a drab and diligent lawyer, with little cutesy collars like Four Court Library collars and a drab hairstyle with bangs down her head and a pudding haircut and who had two (election) outings which hadn't worked and had shown absolutely no evidence, not only that she had the charisma to project herself as she did towards the end of the campaign, but that she would even tolerate it being done - that she would allow herself to use her body, and it was used - her sexuality was a critical part, her whole charisma and appearance - there was no evidence that any of that was going to happen or that she would allow it to happen."

Robinson received the party nomination on 26 April and the campaign was formally launched five days later on May Day.

Again, the nomination received sparse coverage, with *The Irish Times*, Robinson's own 'constituency' newspaper, relegating it to page 17.

The image she presented that day was still of a candidate with roots and affiliations firmly on the left-liberal side of the political spectrum. She was photographed flanked by members of the Labour Party, the Workers' Party, by Jim Kemmy who had just joined the Labour Party and by members of trade union and women's groups.

In statements, Spring promised a "united left campaign" which would shake the political establishment to its roots. Kemmy added his piece stating that the public were looking to the left for leadership on issues such as emigration and jobs.

At this stage it was clear that the Labour Party had their own separate agenda for the campaign. Promoting Robinson could indeed reopen the liberal-progressive agenda, shake up the political establishment, brush the cobwebs from the office of President, but a successful campaign could also boost the party in the next Local elections and have a knock-on effect in the next General Election.

Since the 1989 election, Labour had been gaining ground on Fine Gael under the abysmal leadership of Alan Dukes, and also on the Workers' Party.

That party had fought an excellent General Election, increasing their TDs from three to seven. They now had six TDs in Dublin compared to Labour's three. But they too had had difficulty matching Dick Spring's performances in the Dáil.

Spring knew that a good performance from Robinson could further enhance his party's status and secure Labour's dominance over the Workers' Party.

According to a Labour Party activist: "It would be the first national election (in recent times) to be fought on a three-corner basis, Fianna Fáil, Fine Gael and Labour, with the Workers' Party in a supporting role and the Progressive Democrats sidelined. It was an opportunity to assert the leadership of the left, with a chance, at the very least, of beating Fine Gael into second place ... and it was a dry run for the local elections, to test our appeal and flex our muscle. "

"Labour's agenda," said a member of the Robinson kitchen cabinet, hostile to Labour's role throughout the campaign, "was to maximise the June '91 (local election) vote. They tried to use her purely for their own purposes and they never saw her as a winner. They were also determined to exclude (from a central role) the Workers' Party and the Greens as well as the Independents."

Whatever about the Greens and Independents, the Labour Party was certainly out to sideline the Workers' Party. They wanted their support, to avoid embarrassing inter-party spats during the election, but they wanted them away from central control, shadows on the margins who, they hoped, would reap little electoral benefit from the campaign.

Prior to Robinson's nomination Spring had made deliberately half-hearted attempts to meet with De Rossa, paying lip service to the idea of a united left candidate with no desire to give De Rossa more than minimal involvement in either the nomination process and the subsequent campaign. Despite repeated attempts by De Rossa to arrange a meeting, it never took place.

"He calculated very simply," says a Workers' Party (WP) TD, "that we weren't in a position to nominate a candidate ourselves therefore he had us."

Labour Party members say their reluctance to take the WP on board stemmed from "our historical experience of working with the Workers' Party on joint campaigns such as the two referenda. They operate on classic stalinist terms, they either want control or they want to set up their own campaign. We didn't need them to nominate her, we had twenty Oireachtas members plus Kemmy. We had a position of advantage which we weren't going to devalue by a co-nomination. We had to play it to maximum effect. Collaborating with the WP would have been inexplicable to Labour supporters outside Dublin especially. In Dublin there was a desire to work with them in some constituencies simply to keep abreast of them. We wanted them on board but not getting too involved. In the words of Lyndon Johnson it was better to have them inside the tent pissing out.

The Workers' Party were keenly aware of the Labour strategy.

"I think what Dick was in the business of doing," said one WP member, "was relaunching the Labour Party and putting as much distance between us and the Labour Party as he possibly could. I think there were two agendas - I think what he was at was to find a Labour Party candidate who would serve two purposes; one was to see us off and the other was to see his own internal left wing off."

On the surface, with the Workers' Party rowing in behind Mary Robinson, a popular choice for its members given their mutual opposition to the Anglo-Irish Agreement when it was first signed, there was harmony between the two parties. But tensions bubbled furiously underneath throughout the entire campaign, with much of the energy of both Bride Rosney and the Labour Party Director of Elections Ruairí Quinn being used to sort out rows between rival Party members in constituencies throughout the country, rows at times degenerating into farce with WP and Labour Party activists fighting over who stood where on a rostrum or who was organising what dinner dance or whose name should be on the letterhead and later coming to Rosney or Quinn like children with cut knees asking them to make it better.

But that was in the future. At this early post-nomination stage, Robinson and Rosney were anxious to get as many people on board as possible, to elicit support from every political organisation, pressure group and community organisation going.

The Workers' Party may have had a low share of the national vote, 4%, but Proinsías De Rossa (with the not insubstantial help of Eoghan Harris) had topped the poll in Dublin in the 1989 European Elections, with over 125,000 first preference votes. They were also a major force in Dublin with twice as many TDs as Labour and the significance of all of this was not lost on the Robinsons.

Within days of the tentative 4 April nomination, Mary Robinson wrote a personal letter to De Rossa asking for support. This she got, once the nomination was 'formalised.'

*

Meanwhile Robinson was about to get another gift from the Workers' Party in the shape of its long time ideologue Eoghan Harris. Three weeks prior to Robinson's nomination, Harris had effectively been forced out of the party following the 'unauthorised' publication of his document *The Necessity of Social Democracy*, a plea to the party to leapfrog Labour and take up the social democratic mantle before they did.

Harris was and is a hugely controversial figure because of his passionate political commitments and his overweaning sense of his own importance. In conversation Harris is dazzling, electric, magnificently arrogant, spewing ideas with pace, humour and clarity.

In Lelia Doolin's classic 1969 book on RTE, *Sit Down and Be Counted: The Cultural Revolution of a Television Station*, she wrote:

> (Harris) had made an impact on the station almost from the moment of joining it as a trainee Producer-Director in 1966, at the age of twenty-four. He had had a brilliant scholastic career and had taught history at University College, Cork. His early and lasting preoccupation was with the revitalising of the Irish spirit - at first romantically under the influence of some of Corkery's students. This gradually gave way to a reflective realism that many of his former associates found harsh and unpalatable. He had a social commitment to the underprivileged of such intensity that it often frightened his friends as much as his opponents.
>
> Of extraordinarily high intelligence among men who were themselves markedly above average, he had nothing of the intellectual bully in his make up.
>
> Fearless of personal consequences, a master of savage irony in both Irish and English, he disturbed the complacent, amused the dilettante and alarmed the plodder. He was born to be a leader. He would always have followers.

One of the major talking points after the election was just how crucial Harris was to the Robinson victory. Harris himself thinks he was critical to the campaign, the catalyst that fused the chemistry of Mary Robinson with that of the electorate. Ask Harris for his verdict on his role and he'll say with customary modesty, "Well Mary and Nick's nickname for me was God."

After the election Harris widely publicised his campaign role, because he claimed he had not been given the credit he deserved in Labour Party and other accounts of the campaign. His blatant self-publicity enraged many in the Party. But negative statements about Harris after the election did not reflect the enormous admiration they had for his work during the campaign.

"The Labour Party were in thrall to him," said a Workers' Party TD, "I had a pain in my arse (listening to them) ... it was Eoghan phoned me this morning and he's said this, or Eoghan has had another idea, he's gone up on the mountain to think, or, Brenda said this to Eoghan and Eoghan is on the phone and Eoghan rang again and Eoghan has a whole new idea and Eoghan this, that and the other, they were fascinated by him. Fergus Finlay (Spring's adviser and press officer) used to come up to me in the canteen in the Dáil and he couldn't wait to bring up the subject about Eoghan, do you know what Eoghan said last night ... it was really something."

But people on all sides of the campaign acknowledge Harris as a "genius", "fucking brilliant", "like no one the Robinsons had ever met before", "breathtaking", while still maintaining reservations about his importance to the campaign. His three 'party political broadcasts', the last one to the strains of a crackling old 75rpm recording of *Nessun Dorma*, hailed as a classic, were inspired. Mary Robinson has said that Harris was "deeply significant at the beginning of the campaign."

But at the beginning was the letter. And the blueprint.

On 5 April, as Harris first read of the Robinson nomination, he was a man at a crossroads, his ties severed with the party he had been involved with for twenty-five years, wearying of RTE, and looking for something to make sense of those two and a half decades and to prove, he said, that he could deliver the social democratic constituency that he had promised to deliver to the Workers' Party who had now rejected him.

To Harris, social democracy was the political framework in which he thought Robinson should campaign.

"Social Democracy in this new Irish sense," he wrote later, "would have three marks: it would be European, accept the north as a separate state, accept the market but with social controls, be fiscally conservative but Keynesian in times of recession, be liberal but not leftie in social and sexual legislation."

On 6 April Harris wrote to Robinson:

Dear Mary,
Congratulations on taking up the Presidential challenge with determination. As a long-time admirer of

yours - especially on the issue of pluralism and Northern Ireland - I wish you all the best.

I want to give you some practical help. What I do is deal with mass media. For the past ten years my small media group created the 'image' of the Workers' Party. Given the Party's past it should be clear that I would have to be the best in the business. Which quite simply I am, not because I understand media, but because I understand the political framework in which media must work - something Saatchi and Saatchi got wrong for Fianna Fáil last election.

One of the reasons I did well for the Workers' Party was because I was given control from the centre. This was critical. You need the same control. Media messers are ten a penny. Most are wrong. You have to have a tiny team, a clear strategy, and stick to it.

The hard decisions come first. What I call Beecher's Brook. Your Beecher's is divorce and abortion. Get it right and you can beat Lenihan in my view. Get it wrong, or worse, mess around, and you are dead.

Let me give you a model of what I mean:

The 1989 General Election and European Election was a classic media campaign by the Workers' Party. The Beecher's Brook decision was to accept the 'market' - a decision made as far back as the 1989 April Ard Fheis for which I wrote De Rossa's U-turn speech. The election media campaign kept up that modernising momentum, from stylish, summery television broadcasts that eschewed socialist jargon in favour of populist lines like 'Our motto is - if it works pay it properly!' right down to the 'green' subtext of the slogan 'A Breath of Fresh Air' and the smoky 'fashion' photos of De Rossa.

Let me stress that the 'dialectics' of the poster photo were critical. Any fool can think up a green slogan. The political point of the poster was that the Pigeon House chimneys were belching smoke in the background *(Author's note: In fact the Pigeon House chimneys emit water vapour, steam, not smoke)* a signal that we were not Dublin 4 green loonies, that we could live with generating stations, that we accepted that some smoke is part of the working life of a modern city. In political terms it had a gritty appeal to workers while holding down the 'green' vote.

This poster, this subliminal signal that we lived in the real world, is what I mean by a political media campaign. All these details are critical. It was critical that De Rossa should wear his jacket slung over his shoulder. That's why he, a relatively unknown leader of three months, headed the poll in Dublin. You can't do that without a brilliant media campaign.

A media campaign must be a marriage of content and form. De Rossa's 1989 Ard Fheis speech calling for acceptance of the market was no more, and no less important than any other contribution such as the slogan 'A Breath of Fresh Air' or the decision to use Mike Bunn - a 'fashion' photographer in trade terms but known to me as a nature photographer too. And I had to fight off messers on election committees who wanted to take out a TV broadcast line of mine: 'We're not dogmatic socialists, we're democratic socialists', because ten days before Tiananmen Square I believed Deng would use force. I was right. If I did not understand politics, if I was just a media 'technician' that vital line would have been left out. Or again I fought for the line 'Our motto is - if it works pay it properly' because it moved forward to welcome entrepreneurial activity rather than just begrudgingly accepting it *à la* Michael D Higgins and Co. Half measures are fatal in media matters.

I tell you all this because you have some hard choices to make and one of them is not to listen to every Tom, Dick and Harry - and especially Dublin 4 dicks. On your team you need some who are racy, of the soil, who have a feel for Catholic cultural mores, who are at home at a noisy Fine Gael function, who could watch a hurling match with relish and know who Packy Bonner is.

My view is that you can win the campaign, or come so close as to give you a famous political victory, by presenting yourself as a democratic rather than a liberal candidate and never as a liberal-left candidate.

Politically you have huge ground to make up. You must secure the entire Fine Gael vote - which you can't do unless you deal with the Distortion issue (Divorce and Abortion). You need to split the Fianna Fáil vote which you can do by pulling their progressive women voters away by a bravura campaign. You need Labour / Dublin 4 / Divorce / Abortion / Rape Crisis / Incest and all that like a hole in the head. You have that.

Right now you have a whole country to win. This does not mean compromising your principles. But it does mean accepting that every morning we invent a new world. In politics you need to put previous political personae aside and start fresh. People like fresh starts.

Finally, in offering you practical help I want to make my status clear. I will not be going back to the Workers' Party, or joining Labour, or any other party. The media team - which left the WP with me - means to devote itself to single issue campaigns on progressive issues such as Peace and Northern Ireland. We are happy to do what we can and meet you whenever you like.

On an upbeat note I met Paul Durcan for a political chat today. He asked me what I thought of you. I said what I thought. He was pleased because he said he had written to you supportively. I thought it a good omen.

Eoghan Harris.

The objective of the campaign, as outlined in the letter, according to Harris, was "to ignore the Labour vote which was hers anyway, and secure the whole of the Fine Gael transfer vote, and hopefully in passing split the Fianna Fáil vote if possible by tapping on certain nerves. The strategy of the campaign as outlined was that Mary should present herself as 'a democratic' rather than a liberal candidate and never as a liberal left candidate ... These words have concrete consequences, two in particular. To secure the Fine Gael vote she would have to say she was a Catholic in the crunch and deny she was a socialist."

Robinson telephoned Harris within days, telling him they clearly had things to talk about and inviting him to her Ranelagh home. To the Robinsons and to Rosney the letter had made an awful lot of sense. Furthermore it had come from someone who could produce results and from the first person who had said out straight that Mary could win. Other observers have noted that the letter and subsequent blueprint appealed to Robinson's intellectual sense of her own importance. Here was someone not only confirming it but pointing a path to the realisation of a destiny she felt she had.

Some days later Harris arrived at the Robinson home, clutching his campaign blueprint. Neither the Robinsons nor Rosney had met Harris before. He dazzled them, talking for hours, giving a virtuoso display of political and media insight and analysis with such confidence that all of them, but especially Nick Robinson, knew he had to come on board.

The document read:

> The makings of Mary Robinson's media campaign. The essence of which is to understand the importance of a preposition.
>
> Take the word 'for' below.
>
> There is a difference between 'A President of All the People' and 'A President for All the People.' The difference is that the first one is Dublin 4 and do-gooding and the second is democratic.
>
> There is no need to talk down. But the mark of a democrat is to seek out the 'fors'.
>
> The first mark of a 'for' person is a sense of humour. You must be serious enough not to take yourself solemnly.
>
> From first to last you must set out to enjoy this campaign. And be seen to enjoy it.
>
> And why not? This is a 'Discover Ireland' trip. Every so often we have to get to know our changing country all over again.
>
> Go out in that spirit of adventure and zest and the sheer energy will enthuse the electorate.
>
> That's something Lenihan can't match. Sheer energy and stamina. So hit the road ...
>
> Every campaign has two Beecher's Brooks for some reason. One is always political. The other is always personal.
>
> The personal issue is an easy jump. You have a plummy Dublin 4 lawyery image. You can fix that easy enough - and the rest of my notes are about how to fix it.

But before that you must jump the big one, the Beecher's Brook that cuts you off from more than half the electorate and which you must jump without any fluffs.

The political fence in the Presidential race is the divorce and abortion issue. Call it the Distortion issue. Call the problem voter Carmel Murphy.

Carmel Murphy* is a bank manager's wife, Cork Bourgeoisie, Jack Lynch voter, progressive but a Catholic in the Cork sense. She says : 'I'd vote for Mary Robinson only for her position on abortion.'

Now you can't mess around with this. Either you deal with it up front or it is no use even starting the campaign. What you have here is a Jack Kennedy problem - and of course a John F Kennedy solution too.

Your very first press conference must deal with Distortion in a frank and firm fashion as follows: 'Now I want to make something clear. Everybody knows my position on divorce and abortion. But that was Mary Robinson's position. As President I will fully accept the views of the electorate expressed at the referenda. On this I compare my position to John F Kennedy - as President of Ireland I represent the views of the people of Ireland. On every issue. Including divorce and abortion. As President my private views don't count ...'

You must say that every chance you get for a whole week and you will never have to say it again. If you don't say it first, and without fidgets, and without fiddling you are a non-runner in this race.

Do it right and you get Carmel Murphy's* vote.

Mary Robinson is cool and competent. But she needs a warmer image. The common touch. That's about it.

Television, as ever, is what counts. This time more than ever. Paradoxically Mary's image of integrity, which comes from *The Irish Times* so to speak, can come across as a cold, Garret Fitzgerald 'mission to explain' persona which is death at the polls. Explaining things is fine for Dublin 4, but a problem nationally.

Not a real person

Alan Dukes is still struggling with his cold fish image. Fine Gael never seems to grasp that intellect is intimidating, so they continue to lack the common touch.

Mary Robinson's current image is one of integrity and intellect - but this is somewhat discounted by cool and competence which sometimes comes across as aloofness in a country which paradoxically values both cool and the common touch, each in its own place. The Parnell factor, the mixture of aloofness and affection is the ideal for candidates for public office in Ireland.

Television can warm up Mary's persona without compromising her three basic strengths: character, calm and competence. But we need cool, not cold.

This has nothing to do with what she says. It is a problem of 'form' not content. Mary needs more 'policies' like a hole in the head. Mary is articulate enough as it is. Now she needs more 'silences'. She needs to be seen listening, what Meryl Streep calls 'listening and thinking and letting them see you do it.'

What Mary needs most of all is for the plain people of Ireland to like her as much as they respect her.

Mary's image of integrity and intellect can be taken as given, they are part of her received image. Any classic picture of her in classic clothes conveys this.

To this must be added a strong 'feminine' factor. Simply stated her image must be softened - caring and compassion must be added to competence and cool, and her image needs much larger doses of the latter.

Start with her non-intellectual and 'character' strengths. She looks good. She looks like she could look soft and caring - when she's off-duty so to speak.

This is the subtext of any media campaign for Mary:

Mary must come across as a person who would make a great President. Dublin 4 subtext question: Why? Because she has the brains for it. Plain People subtext: Why? Because she has the beauty for it - she'd make us look good. General subtext question: Tell us why? Because she's the kind of competent, compassionate, caring and attractive woman we would like our wife / daughter / sister / mother / girlfriend to be if we are men;

and the kind of woman we want to be if we are women - and remember women's images of the ideal are also reflections of how men view that ideal too.

For women Mary should be the kind of woman they want to be; for men the kind of woman they would like to be seen with in public, or to talk to in private.

THE TWIN PRONGS OF A PRESIDENTIAL CAMPAIGN

The twin prongs of a campaign should be posters and photo-opportunities. The posters should be presidential. The photo moments - which are always aimed at television first - should be strongly feminine and stress her informal and democratic instincts.

This contrast must be pointed by dress and deportment - presidential posters with classic clothes; photo/tv ops in summery dresses, casual raincoats, slung bags etc.

THE PURPOSE OF THE PHOTO/TV OPS

There is no need to fake anything. Mary Robinson has a strong track record on women's issues. What's needed is to take the 'issue' out of these ideas and put people back at the centre. Put aside the 'mission to explain', the over-articulation of 'problems' in terms of precedent and procedure, the L and H boredom of summoning up previous malpractices of Fianna Fáil (what I call in RTE training courses The Fatal Tyranny of Fine Gael Fact) and instead talk about moving on.

But not just talk - for television you must really move.

Mary must be seen on the move, meeting the right people, almost always with a caring dimension - which is not the same as a Michael D Higgins 'pity the poor whores' dimension. Nobody ever won an election on pity. Only by promising an end to the need for it.

Mary must visit community clinics - but clinics which are full of fight back. One of the classic errors of the hard left is not to understand a simple piece of psychology: ordinary people are full of pity - but they hate whiners. So Mary should visit Rape Crisis centres -

but stress the positive. She must visit mental hospitals - but where we see things done so well that we don't grudge a call for more cash. She must visit the disabled - but disabled on the move, disabled who are fighting back, the Gene Lambert type, fighters and full of hope, only needing a figurehead, a President who is not afraid to be seen with people in need, but people who need hope as well as hard cash.

GENERAL AIMS
Posters and photo ops do different - and this must be faced - dialectically contradictory jobs. This contradiction is in my view the dialectical secret of making use of mass media. The poster's aim is to create confidence in her ability and authority to do the job. The photo ops aim is paradoxically almost to contradict this by softening the way she goes about it, by creating confidence, not so much in her 'macho' ability to see it through but to give people a subliminal signal that she would not be rigid about the rules as a man would, that she would not hesitate to break Presidential rectitude to pick up a crying child. So while it must convey that she can do the job it must also convey that she would do it with compassion - simply stated we must never forget that she is a woman.

CLOTHES
Pictures, especially television pictures, determine modern voting. Clothes are critical. You cannot spend too much on good clothes. Classy and classless clothes that speak softly. Ian Galvin at Brown Thomas has a gift for clothes for cameras. Take his advice and don't blink at the bill. It is money well spent.

FINAL WORD OF ADVICE
Whenever a camera points at you - think hard about a real problem. Focus on it. Nod imperceptibly as you solve it. Let them see you do it ...

THE CRUCIAL CONSTITUENCY
Munster is the one to win. This is fertile territory for you. Michael Collins Powell ran a brilliant campaign

here for Tom O'Higgins years ago and that feeling
against Fianna Fáil under Haughey is there. Cox tapped
into it last year. You must spend twice as long in
Munster. You must conjure up the Jack Lynch factor in
Cork by hitting Blackpool. Go into Béal na mBlath and
Bandon and Michael Collins country. Clonmel, Cashel
and all those towns are worth investing time in. Munster
can make all the difference to what your final tally looks
like.

CAMPAIGN LOGOS

You need distinctive, attractive European colour systems
for posters and logos. Colour is critical. Think of the
way Peter Mandelson used the red rose in Britain. You
need a 'feminine' but strong colour system, preferably
Italian style with a typography designed by a graphic
artist with a feel for that kind of 'soft' political attack.

CAMPAIGN SONGS

For TV and radio a gentle version of the Zoological
Gardens. For cars with speaker systems there should be a
version of 'Mrs Robinson' with a few new simple lyrics.
Nobody really remembers its risqué film connotations
and if they did it would be a plus.

TV AND RADIO BROADCASTS

Like this. Gentle rollicking version of 'Did you ever go
up to the Phoenix Park' or whatever. Pictures of you,
looking Presidential in a Paul Costello suit at Law
Library, Dáil, National Library, Collins statue Cork,
Galway city, Airports, Dublin castle. All intercut with
summery pix of you in coat and scarves, moving round
streets, schools, clinics, smiling, shaking hands, listening
a lot, nodding a lot, and above all surrounded by people.
No commentary. Just a few lines at the end from a very
male voice.

NEWSPAPERS

I put this after 'clothes' to make a point. Newspaper press
releases have no effect on a modern election. The
function of a press release is mainly to keep the pot
boiling, to authenticate what you say for Sean Duignan

on *Six One*. Newspapers have two important functions
1. To follow the Presidential tour with feature articles.
2. To offer codes of cultural conduct. You do not need anybody to read what you say. But it is critical what paper your picture appears in most often. The very fact that you are in the *Sunday Independent* reassures devout Catholics even if they never read a word. Contrariwise if you appear in colour in the *Sunday Tribune* more than once Carmel Murphy* will see it on the stand and mark you down as a Dublin 4 Tribune type. (Remember the Tribune has a tiny circulation and its covers are a cultural code for a certain kind of lefty trendy type [...]). Sunday newspapers matter most. The newspaper you need every week is the *Sunday Independent* with a million readers - and whose endorsement reassures everybody you are not anti-Catholic. Vital too is *The Sunday Press* to pull in the Jack Lynch and the populist vote. And it goes without saying that you have to crack the *Sunday World* which is a paper I respect because it is what it is [...] and always delivers good features to me. *The Irish Times* you have - and a poisoned chalice it can be too. Mind the *Irish Press* whose journalists have much better politics [...] and the *Irish Independent*. Further, you need to nurse selected papers ... [which] will set out to destroy you unless you remind them of a Fine Gael dimension. From that you can deduce that you need a Fine Gael godfather, in short you need the imprimatur of Garret Fitzgerald.

THE CAMPAIGN BUS
This election will be won by the Pat Cox factor. I mean you get into a bus on day one and you stay in it, hitting town after town, at a steady remorseless pace, running Lenihan ragged, like Sheridan going down the Shenandoah valley, leaving nothing but scorched earth behind for Lenihan.

THE SURPRISE FACTOR
Surprise is the key to victory. Everybody will expect Mary Robinson to run a dignified loser's campaign.

*Not a real person

What they will not expect and what the public will delight in is if Mary Robinson runs a barnstorming, bus-pounding, no holds barred, will to win, old style political campaign that leaves Lenihan panting.

That will take enormous energy. Mary has that energy.

What's needed now is the will to win.

The blueprint was lapped up by those in the room.

"I went through the blueprint," says Harris, "It was pure pleasure to see how fast Mary made it her own. Sex at its best is nothing on a meeting of true minds. Bride of course is a political animal of the first order and knew it was the goods. But Nick was the revelation. He seemed to soak it through his skin ... but what made a real difference was the background of the row over my pamphlet *The Necessity of Social Democracy*. All those present had read it and Bride Rosney in particular understood its implications for image-making. But the most important factor at that crucial meeting was Mary Robinson herself. Her sense of purpose was palpable."

Harris himself was surprised at Robinson's confidence, at times bordering on arrogance, that not only did she feel she could win but that if she did win she would make a great President.

One observer describes her confidence as "the arrogance of her class". Others believe that Robinson did see herself as a woman with a mission, something which Nick Robinson also sensed in Mary, compelling him to take a subordinate role in their public life, a man who acted at times, say those on the campaign, more as a consort than a husband.

For Rosney the most crucial element in the Harris document was his plan for the 'enactment' of the campaign, that it should be a seven month stretch, that it should have three acts and that it should start immediately. Many of the issues he outlined, the Robinsons and Rosney had already discussed themselves. What Harris had done was provide them with a set of solutions to the problems they knew they had - Robinson's narrowly based appeal, the 'Beecher's Brook' of abortion and divorce, and how to eat into 'Indian territory' - the Fianna Fáil and Fine Gael constituencies.

Meetings with Harris took place throughout the rest of the

month with Harris setting up shop in Sandford Road and the Robinsons and Rosney, like students in a lecture theatre, frantically keeping pace with him as he lectured all three on his theory of communication and discussed campaign policies.

Out of this, says Harris, came the idea of a 'working President', notions of 'empowering' community groups, ideas of the Presidency as a stimulus for excellence in all fields.

That the Robinsons and Rosney believed that Mary could win is not in doubt - that they were also prepared to be ruthless to achieve victory is also indisputable.

During the early part of the campaign Robinson had gathered together a group of influential women friends and activists who came to meetings at her home to act as a policy sounding board. They included Frances Gardner (WPA), Frances Fitzgerald (CSW), Dr Mary Henry, Dr Maura Woods, Niamh Breathnach, Ita O'Connor, journalists Mairin de Burca, Mary Holland, Nuala O'Faolain, Nell McCafferty, Mary Maher, Mary Cummins and Kate Shanahan, Rita Burtenshaw (Dublin Well Woman Centre), Anna Lee, Grainne Farren and Nuala Feric (Cherish), Barbara Hussey, Maire Bates, Ann O'Donnell (formerly of the Dublin Rape Crisis Centre) and Mary Higgins (Threshold).

After the second meeting, two of the journalists approached Robinson suggesting that she appoint Ann O'Donnell as her press officer. Robinson agreed enthusiastically and approached O'Donnell about the job, who was also enthusiastic.

But Bride Rosney was totally opposed, telling Robinson that O'Donnell was too identified with a single issue and this would damage Mary who needed to be identified with a much broader based set of policies.

Of course choosing Ann O'Donnell, former PRO of the Anti-Amendment Campaign in 1983, would also have raised Harris's Beecher's Brook 'Distortion' issue. O'Donnell was identified not just with the single issue of rape crisis counselling but also with campaigns on issues which the Robinson team, while not deliberately steering clear of, were not exactly pushing to the forefront either. Appointing O'Donnell would, it was argued, have evoked public memories of the two divisive referenda campaigns in which Robinson herself had played a very active role.

Taking Rosney's advice Robinson canvassed several more

people for their view. They told her she was crazy, that O'Donnell had an established profile of controversial referenda involvement in which her side lost. In actual fact, Ann O'Donnell had been prominent only in the Anti-Amendment Campaign, and not in the Divorce referendum. But the reason for not appointing her remained valid - she brought with her the whiff of electoral failure. Rosney urged Robinson that what she needed instead was the aura of success.

Two days after her first approach to O'Donnell Robinson phoned her again to say she would not be requiring her services. O'Donnell was reportedly deeply hurt but the only media account of this, although it was known to a number of women journalists, appeared in *Phoenix* magazine and was never taken up by other publications.

In fact many of the women in that early kitchen cabinet were incensed at the treatment of O'Donnell erroneously thinking that it was the male members of the formal campaign team, and not Rosney who had vetoed the appointment. Though disllusioned, they refused to go public on the incident, a stance which characterised much of the campaign. While many of the more radical feminist Robinson supporters were annoyed at the back burner position of some of the controversial issues Robinson had campaigned for in the past, they held back from public comment for fear of damaging a campaign which they saw as hugely beneficial to their causes in the long run.

One recalled willing Robinson to declare her deep devotion to the Catholic faith when questioned about faith and morals on a *Today Tonight* programme. And Robinson did. Harris, after all, had recommended this approach in his blueprint.

Many of the women activists involved in the campaign, Labour Party workers and others, admired Mary Robinson, and Rosney, hugely. But few related well to the two women on a personal level. Some actively disliked both. Despite the new, warmer image of the campaign, Robinson at times came across as cerebral, distant and cold.

When Eoghan Harris's great friend and former Workers' Party colleague Eamon Smullen died during the campaign while on holidays, Harris was struck by the fact that neither Mary, Nick or Bride commiserated on his loss.

Brenda O'Hanlon was eventually chosen as public relations

person. She was an enormously energetic and successful public relations consultant, then working for the prestigious Wilson Hartnell PR company. O'Hanlon, always immaculately and expensively dressed, had no whiff of failure about her and, in her designer clothes, evoked no stereotyped 'negative' images of feminist agitation. She resigned from Wilson Hartnell - her salary during the campaign was paid for privately by the Robinsons.

*

Homework done, on 30 April, Robinson set out on the campaign trail. Her first port of call, as far away from her Dublin urban base as possible, was to a preparatory conference on peripheral communities in Allihies in south west Cork, a near perfect spot to begin throwing off the urban image, to mix with the 'real Ireland' in the face of Atlantic gales.

The picture that subsequently appeared of Robinson in *The Irish Times*, showed her facing windwards, hair blown back, resting against a small fishing boat. Already the old 'lawyery' urban image was crumbling ...

The initial tour, largely coastal, lasted until July. It was tentative, Mary and Nick largely on their own, establishing as many contacts as they could from every interest group and organisation they could, occasionally joined by members of the Labour Party. Both the Robinsons and Rosney felt that the Party considered that a 'real campaign' lasts for six weeks and that there was little point in putting their backs into it before then.

The tour also helped to hone Robinson's policies. She abandoned an early 'constitutional change' proposal in favour of extolling an expanded Presidency but within the parameters of the Constitution. A theme began to emerge - self-help and development, giving a voice to groups who were 'fighting back' in the face of massive disadvantage and unemployment.

The tour, though sparsely covered in the national media, laid down a base, a network of support, a bulwark against any candidate Fine Gael might put forward. Her visits to various towns and villages did get coverage in the provincial press and Robinson was astounded at the penetration of the new local radio stations.

By the time she went on holidays in August Mary Robinson felt she had covered a lot of ground, literally and figuratively. Her ideas had crystalised. What the people wanted was a 'recognition factor', someone who would, in a phrase she heard over and over again, 'do us proud.'

She would clock up between 15,000-20,000 miles before the other two candidates were even in the field. This early campaign would also serve to help her weather the 'red' smear and the 'distortion' factor later in the campaign. The ordinary people of Ireland had seen her, and seen that she did not have horns.

And, as she went on holidays, buoyed by her reception around the country, at least one newspaper had treated her candidacy as more than simply nominal. In a poll carried out at the end of May by Lansdowne Market Research for *The Sunday Business Post*, Robinson had been tested against potential candidates in Fianna Fáil and Fine Gael. The research agency, in its summary, had noted one key factor:

> Robinson is clearly capable of pulling in Fine Gael votes, even against Fitzgerald. Against a lesser Fine Gael candidate Robinson could move ahead and become the main rival to Lenihan.

The Robinson campaign began again in earnest towards the middle of September. August had been an anxious time, waiting for the Fine Gael candidate to emerge. The prospect of Carmencita Hederman emerging either for Fine Gael, or endorsed by Independents and possibly the PDs, was 'a nightmare' - a direct clash with Robinson on many issues and diluting the novelty value and appeal of a woman candidate.

But an even more nightmarish scenario, as far as Bride Rosney was concerned, was the prospect of Fine Gael abandoning plans to run their own candidate and rowing in behind Robinson instead. In a two horse race, she felt certain, Robinson would have no chance against Lenihan. They needed Proportional Representation, they needed a second count and those vital second preferences.

It was a relief when Currie was nominated. They knew he'd come third.

*

September saw endless squabbles between Labour and the Workers' Party. Eamon Gilmore, Workers' Party TD for Dun Laoghaire, made repeated attempts to get on the campaign committee, and Ruairí Quinn and others did their level best to keep him off, arguing that since the Workers' Party had launched their own campaign for Mary Robinson they had no need to be on theirs. Gilmore finally gained his committee seat on 10 October, less than a month before the election. When he did, Quinn set up a new core group that met apart from the main committee. Gilmore was excluded.

Tensions were also running high between the Robinsons and the Labour Party with both sides keeping to their own, private, agendae - Labour's to keep a very public and definite link with the candidate and Bride Rosney's to do her best to sever that link as far as politically practicable in the public mind. Undoubtedly influenced by Harris's view of the Party as 'a bunch of losers' who wanted nothing more than a good second place performance from Robinson, Rosney regarded most of their actions with suspicion, seeing much of their work as amateurish. In the early days she had battled against the 'Labour nominee' tag. In an ideal world she would have preferred Robinson to be presented as, simply, 'the candidate Mrs Robinson.' What really maddened Rosney was when Robinson was tagged in the media as 'the candidate of the Left.'

She lost few opportunities to criticise individual Labour members. When Spring announced that he would accompany Robinson to London to meet with Irish emigrants, Rosney let everyone know that in her opinion Spring was only going because his Kerry North constituency rival, Jimmy Deenihan, had accompanied Austin Currie on a similar trip. She also complained about pressure from the party to send Robinson to places where Labour was weak.

Rosney also tried to ensure that both Labour and the Workers' Party would be represented at functions attended by the candidate. On one occasion Robinson was invited to a dinner dance in Wexford which Rosney and the Robinsons assumed was a broad-based function. In fact it was organised by Wexford Labour TD Brendan Howlin, and the information was quickly relayed to Rosney back in Dublin by WP member Mick Enright.

Rosney immediately contacted Robinson, already en route to Wexford, by car phone urging her to go to Whites Hotel first to meet with a Workers' Party group. In effect, two separate programmes had to be arranged that night, just to keep everybody happy. The whole thing ended in sheer farce with a cavalcade of supporters' cars, and the Robinsons, stuck up a cul-de-sac inadvertently led there by the driver in front who was simply going home. The night was rounded off with a screaming telephone row between Brendan Howlin and Bride Rosney which reportedly ended in a draw.

Ruairí Quinn was forced to sort out his own party in Meath where the older brigade were vociferously objecting to younger members getting involved with the Workers' Party to form a broadly-based Pro-Robinson front. They dropped their objections only after Quinn told them that the campaign would have a positive knock-on effect for their candidate-in-waiting, Brian Fitzgerald.

It was Robinson herself who had insisted on widespread Workers' Party involvement despite Labour Party entreaties that they only had 4% of the poll, that their involvement would be counterproductive and all they needed to do was get their own vote out.

Typical of the missives received by Rosney in connection with the inter-party feud was one in early September from the regional administrator of the Workers' Party in Cork, John Jefferies.

> A Chara,
>
> I am writing to you regarding the proposed visit of Mary Robinson to Cork tomorrow, Friday. I would be grateful if you could let me know whether tomorrow's visit is being organised by yourselves in the Mary Robinson committee or whether it is by the Labour Party.

Rosney replied :

> Dear Mr Jefferies,
>
> With reference to your fax received in campaign headquarters today, regarding Mary Robinson's visit to Cork tomorrow, the organiser of the programme is Joe

O'Flynn. Although Joe is a member of the Labour Party, he organised the programme on behalf of the campaign committee. We would be delighted if you and members of the Workers' Party would be in attendance at the activities organised.

Robinson herself did as few favours for the Labour Party as possible, greatly to the annoyance and at times distress of Dick Spring who, along with Ruairí Quinn, acted honourably throughout the campaign.

If it hadn't been for him, after all, Robinson would now be sitting in Dublin sifting through files in the Law Library and not whizzing the length and breadth of the country mentally rearranging the furniture in Aras an Uachtaráin.

On one occasion, Workers' Party Director of Elections Pat Rabbitte had accompanied the campaign team and Dick Spring to Ballyhaunis, where Robinson gave a long interview to the local radio station. Rabbitte and Spring sat together in Val's Bar sipping hot whiskeys and listening to the interview.

The interviewer, a woman, was very sharp, getting stuck into the candidate on the issue of rural development and querying why small farmers should vote for her given that the Labour Party had never been seen as a friend of the farmers in the Mayo area.

In reply Robinson said that as everyone well knew she had had nothing to do with the Labour Party for five years and that she was not putting forward, or supporting, Labour Party policies in the election.

Rabbitte winced as she said it, embarrassed for Spring who sat in silence. Eventually the Labour Leader did comment, almost under his breath, "Well damn it," he muttered, "she could have said that we have eight rural TDs."

The other major dilemma at the beginning of the final part of the campaign was the role of Eoghan Harris. Back in April and May, Harris had been content to play a background role, to conceal his work for the Robinsons, because of his employment with RTE. It suited the Robinsons too. When Harris's name was first mentioned in the press, in a short piece by Geraldine Kennedy in *The Irish Times* in late June, just before Harris went on holidays, the Labour Party were enraged.

The Kennedy piece had been brought up for mention at the

following Wednesday's campaign meeting with John Rogers, a close personal friend and adviser to Dick Spring, warning Robinson off, stating that Harris was dangerous, a maverick, that his presence in the campaign would annoy not alone Labour but also the Workers' Party. Rogers, Fergus Finlay and Ruairí Quinn also expressed their disapproval.

But in mid-September, when Harris returned from his holidays, his attitude to his role had changed. He wanted to come out of the closet.

"Immediately I felt a constraint," says Harris, "what they (the Robinsons) had to say was very painful for them to say. Nick told me that Labour had gone ape when they found out about me during the summer. He and Mary were in a dilemma - they wanted me for what they knew would be difficult and dirty weeks. But Labour would not wear it. They left the decision to me. What was facing me was another political campaign in which my work would be kept from public view."

The following day Harris fired off a letter to the Robinsons:

Dear Mary and Nick,
I slept on the problem. And I'm quite clear on what I have to do. Think of it like this: RTE could offer me a deal today or tomorrow. I would then be free to work in your campaign. But it now seems that I would not be acceptable to the Gang of Four...
[...] They should be told to go and fuck themselves. Of course I can see why that's a problem. But I am not going to put myself in a closet.
So count me out if I am in a closet. Naturally I shall do or say nothing that might hurt your campaign. And I am profoundly sorry that I can't carry on. Bride and Peter [MacMenamin] are great people. And of course, politics apart, I like you and Nick a lot, and hate to part like this.

In the end, Nick Robinson squared Harris's involvement with the Labour Party through the great diplomat of the campaign, Ruairí Quinn. Quinn rang Harris, the two men met and from then on the two communicated several times a week. Relations between Harris, Dick Spring and Fergus Finlay were also good for the rest of the campaign.

By late September all three candidates were in the ring and heavy media attention was now focussed on the campaign. Both Fianna Fáil and Fine Gael, through their own private polls, were aware of how well Mary Robinson was doing and were now convinced that she would have no difficulty in coming second.

Her campaign was now largely based in Dublin with occasional forays down the country, giving the impression that she was still conducting a national tour.

The first media outing of the three candidates together, on RTE Radio's *Saturday View*, had gone reasonably well for Robinson, with Lenihan coming off the worst of the encounter, unable to inject any excitement into his vision of the role of the President and already under pressure on the 'independence' issue. The Labour nominated candidate was on a roll.

Then came the 4 October and Robinson's interview in *Hot Press* (an Irish rock magazine) - an apparently thoughtless romp through a myriad of issues, felling holy cows as she went, the Church, the judiciary, family planning inadequacies, homosexuality - nothing was sacred.

The morning papers, thoughtfully provided with extracts from the interview the night before by *Hot Press* who knew they had something very sexy indeed on their hands, gave prominence to her remarks with their reports then carried extensively on *What It Says in the Papers* on RTE 1.

The Irish Times headlined its piece 'Robinson Would Promote Gay Rights'. The report stated that Robinson had said that she would actively support the use of contraceptives and defend the rights of minority groups such as the gay community. The report continued that Robinson had said "yes" when asked if she would perform the official opening of an (illegal) contraceptive stall in the Virgin Megastore. It also quoted her view that "the whole patriarchal, male-dominated presence of the Catholic Church is probably the worst aspect of all the establishment forces that have sought to do down women over the years." She had similar choice views on judges.

With hindsight, members of the Robinson campaign team have said that it was only journalists who got excited by the interview. That was patently not the case. Whatever about the general public, the campaign team themselves were stunned by what she had said, devastated that a major error had been made.

Some weeks earlier, when she had agreed to do the interview, Rosney had warned Robinson that *Hot Press* reporters were adept at dragging out 'the quotable quote'. Robinson assured her she'd be careful, telling her afterwards that the interview had gone well though they had brought up the usual 'Robinson' issues, the Church, family planning and so on.

Rosney first heard of the published interview when she received a call at work from campaign HQ shortly after 8:00pm. Robinson was en route to Kilmacud in south county Dublin at the time. Rosney did not get too alarmed feeling that the whole thing would blow over, that Mary would only get into real trouble if she tried to explain it away.

And that was precisely what Robinson planned to do, agreeing to do an interview with Shane Kenny on RTE Radio *News at One* later that day.

Meanwhile, back at campaign HQ in Merrion Square, Ruairí Quinn had arrived to find a press release in preparation in which Robinson appeared to be denying what she had said on the tape. The spectre of Watergate and cover-up jobs immediately set off alarm bells for Ruarí Quinn. Release nothing, he said.

The *News at One* interview began with Robinson, as predicted by Rosney, now digging herself into a much deeper hole, denying her own words on tape. If the interview had been in court, with Mary as prosecuting barrister, said a Labour TD, she would have been in very deep trouble.

Asked by Kenny to spell out whether she did intend to open illegal contraceptive stalls, such as the one in the Virgin Megastore, Robinson replied: "Yes, I have the text of the interview. I did not say yes at the start of that question. I was asked in what I thought was a kind of trendy way about the Virgin Megastore and I said ... this is a very young country and I think it would be helpful if the President was in touch with what young people are doing ... I would not as President be associated with something that is not legal."

The rest of the interview featured Mary, clearly panicking, attempting to reconstruct the image she had so carefully cultivated during the campaign, an image at odds with the one she had put forward in the magazine interview. She insisted to Kenny that she would use the Aras to promote 'family life', that she had been happily married for 20 years, had three children, and many friends who were priests and nuns, and that she was a Catholic who attended mass and who also brought her children along.

Fortunately for Robinson, within days the whole issue had died a death. Fianna Fáil, still in their 'let's not get the candidate involved in any controversy' mode, made little public play out of the interview, and Fine Gael, for reasons outlined later, also failed to make capital.

What also killed the story was both the apparent unwillingness of the media to hound Robinson on her statements, and the mistaken belief in the public mind that an opinion poll published some days later, which showed Robinson with an impressive 32% of the poll, had been taken *after* the interview and therefore indicated no negative fallout. In fact the poll had been conducted some days before.

And, of course, Robinson's early campaigning had paid off. The new image had set.

"In a word," said a campaign worker, "we got lucky."

Meanwhile, over in Fianna Fáil, luck was something Brian Lenihan and his team could have done with a lot more of.

3
Going Through the Motions

It looked like a mafia funeral with all the big guys in the front row and Lenihan propped up there - one of the lads.

In spring 1990 the RTE *Late Late Show* tribute to Brian Lenihan, described luridly if accurately above by a Fine Gael handler, epitomised the problem which Fianna Fáil would later discover in the Presidential campaign - the show appealed to the Party hard core and sent ripples of distaste through critical sections of the wider electorate.

A few months later, when the votes were counted in the Presidential Election, that's what Lenihan had held - the Party core vote. Those who had earlier toyed with giving the Tánaiste a first or second preference had, after the tapes controversy, legged it back to perceived respectability and Mary Robinson.

The *Late Late Show* tribute evoked echoes of the Party's rakish past, of the men in mohair suits propping up the bars of the nation, plotting their little strokes, wallowing in their scraps of power, exercising it crudely through veiled threats to young Gardaí who happened upon the wrong late night drinking party. They were images of an old-fashioned parochial Ireland which the country's new middle class now found downright embarrassing. What Fianna Fáil supporters saw that night was an affable good old boy. What others saw, said one observer was "an arch 1960s gobshite."

It wasn't altogether fair to Lenihan. If he was to be faulted it was because for too long he had lived up to the Party image, letting his bosses use him as a cross between a court jester and a political band aid.

At least one senior Fine Gael TD believes that Lenihan is one of the most intelligent men in the Dáil, but that through the years he colluded in the Party's abuse of that same intelligence. Former coalition Minister the late John Kelly had once dubbed him The Walking Credibility Gap. But of course anti-intellectualism was almost a core value in Fianna Fáil.

Brian Lenihan's career in Dáil politics ,which began in 1961, had always been entwined with that of Charles J Haughey. In the late 1960's, under the leadership of Sean Lemass, Lenihan and Haughey, along with the late Donogh O'Malley had formed what the late journalist John Healy described as 'an inner cabinet of their own', dubbing the trio 'the three musketeers.'

Lenihan would serve in nine different administrations, becoming in later years celebrated less for his achievements in office, than for his role as Party emollient and Haughey cheerleader. It was Lenihan who did the warm up for Charlie at the annual Party Ard Fheis, Lenihan who interceded with the Boss on behalf of out of favour backbenchers and more senior colleagues, Lenihan who was wheeled out to RTE to pour oil on troubled Fianna Fáil waters with his by now legendary catch phrase, 'No Problem.'

In later years the legend of the great friendship between the two men continued. It wasn't true. They were friends, close enough, but the social circles they moved in were radically different. Haughey befriended the artists, the movers and shakers, the society queens, while Lenihan still knocked back the pints with his old political cronies. The two men had moved apart.

By the late 1980s Brian Lenihan had become more of a doted upon, indulged, national institution than a politician who commanded serious respect. That period coincided with serious health problems, culminating in a liver transplant operation at the Mayo Clinic in Rochester, New York in 1990. It was the friends of Fianna Fáil who rallied round the man at the time, paying the bulk of the medical costs, allowing the family to travel in private jets there and back. It was a reasonable reward for the years of loyal Party service.

Colleagues believe that the operation rehabilitated Lenihan not only physically but politically as well. His post-operation profile was larger than ever. Whatever the man wanted from the Party, the man now had to get.

And Charlie did the business, appointing him as Defence Minister in the 1989 Coalition administration, the least onerous position in Government but a Cabinet post none the less. Some argued much later that Haughey had now done more than enough for the man. But Lenihan still served one vital Party function - political peace maker.

And so, when the smart boys in the Party, Government Press Secretary PJ Mara and Kildare TD Charlie McCreevy among them, wondered how to get the Party through its post-coalition trauma in the autumn of 1989, and stave off a savaging by the grassroots at the next local elections, it was to good old Brian that they turned.

The rationale was faultless. Lenihan, the most popular man in Fianna Fáil, was the one candidate they were unlikely to turn on if he ran for President. Anger would be put to one side to help 'good old Brian' - the grassroots in turn would be boosted by a good election showing and would then be less likely to knife the Party in the back at the local elections.

So the boys set to work, deliberately planting Lenihan's name in selected newspapers columns, creating such a momentum for the idea that when at the annual Fianna Fáil President's dinner in December 1989, CJ Haughey said "he (Lenihan) will still be one of us whatever high office he is called to during the next decade," the hall erupted, believing this to be the Haughey benediction on Lenihan's candidacy.

Lenihan was more than happy to indulge the media speculation. In an *Irish Independent* article on 16 December the Tánaiste was quoted as saying, "I'm very happy in my present job and have no intention of seeking the Presidency, but if it should be offered to me I would consider it a great honour to accept."

Two weeks later he confirmed that he would be available to take up a Fianna Fáil offer of a nomination. "I would be honoured," he said, "as any Irishman would be honoured to run for the Presidency."

By Christmas the Lenihan candidacy was a virtual certainty in the public mind, a fact which both puzzled and worried Haughey who asked PJ Mara how Lenihan had managed to get such a good campaign going.

In fact Haughey, despite the December 'benediction', was now developing cold feet at the prospect of President Lenihan. A win, a racing certainty at this stage, would mean a by-election in Dublin West with a Fianna Fáil victory not at all certain. A defeat would put them technically in a minority position in the

Dáil and threaten Government stability, a nightmarish scenario for Haughey.

After Christmas, Lenihan had become aware that Haughey was cooling on his candidacy. He never discussed the election with his Tánaiste apart from a vague remark that Lenihan should get himself fit for whatever lay ahead.

Through his own Party contacts he learned that Haughey had been having 'consultations' with Party TDs, including Cabinet members, many of whom also had cold feet at the prospect of Lenihan standing. Haughey simply didn't want to know. In late spring, the then Minister for the Marine, Cavan-Monaghan TD John Wilson, also indicated that he too would like to stand, something which further unsettled the Tánaiste and his very anxious family.

Lenihan sensed that there was a definite dampening down of his candidacy with reporters being told that he was not an absolute certainty and some political columnists even speculating that the Taoiseach himself might run.

But there was still widespread expectation that the Lenihan candidacy would be launched at the Party Ard Fheis in April. Nothing happened; and still there was no signal from the leadership as to when it would happen. For a time, at least in public, Lenihan kept the faith, telling *The Sunday Business Post* in mid-April that Haughey was 'a tremendously loyal person to his friends, generous in spirit and a very kind and considerate person in all his personal relationships and dealings.'

But privately he was beginning to have his doubts. He believed that he would receive the nomination in the end, such was the momentum that had been built up and opinion polls in late May also indicated that he was far and away the best bet for Fianna Fáil.

But the dragging of feet by Haughey bothered him.

"During this period," said a friend of Lenihan's, "Brian began to realise the type of man that Haughey really was. After 30 years or whatever it was suddenly a situation was developing where things weren't quite as clear-cut, where there was no official confirmation of when the nomination would take place and in addition stories were circulating that it might not even be Brian."

But during the summer Haughey eventually realised that he

could do nothing to block Lenihan's candidacy. All the advice was that his Tánaiste had built up such a momentum that it would be counterproductive to stop it. There was also a vague possibility, because of the Wilson interest, that he might even be defeated in his bid.

In the end, Wilson did throw his hat into the ring though not before he informed Haughey of what he was doing and Haughey had raised no objections. The result of the tussle between the two men was a clear-cut victory for Lenihan.

After the vote, at a meeting of the Parliamentary Party, Haughey read out a medical report from Lenihan's doctor at the Mater Private Hospital. He told the TDs that the Tánaiste was fit to undertake a normal campaign and to take up the position of President should he win.

What Haughey omitted from the report were the *caveats* the doctor had included, that Lenihan needed to take care of his diet on the campaign, to take his medication, and to have one clear rest period in the day no matter what. There was nothing too alarming in the *caveats* but it was significant that Haughey omitted them, fearing that any hint that Lenihan had to take more than usual care of his health would lead to accusations that the Party was running an invalid for the Park.

When a *Sunday Tribune* reporter later tried to get a copy of the report PJ Mara told her that the public had no "fucking right" to know details of the man's medical condition.

Meanwhile Party headquarters in Mount Street were gearing up for the election. Qualitative research on attitudes to the Presidency and on the prospects for likely candidates had been prepared prior to Lenihan's selection.

The work was conducted by a company called *Behaviour and Attitudes* who also did the Party's private opinion polls throughout the election. Seven candidates were tested for suitability for the office and placed in the following order:

Brian Lenihan	45%
Mary Robinson	24%
Peter Barry	23%
Carmencita Hederman	20%
Austin Currie	10%
Monica Barnes	7%
Jim Dooge	5%

Lenihan, Currie and Robinson polled with Peter Barry in a three-way contest when the main survey was done in August, showing Lenihan with 54% of the vote, Robinson with 26% and Barry with 20%. Polled again in late September, with Currie now in the race, the findings showed a significant increase in Robinson's vote - up 6 points to 32%, with Lenihan dropping five points to 49% and Currie at 19%

The company's commentary on the August findings highlighted a number of factors which would later be seen as crucial to the eventual outcome of the campaign. It highlighted in particular the growing strength of Mary Robinson who had now been campaigning for five months, and the weaknesses in the Currie camp.

It also drew attention to some negative perceptions of Lenihan, perceptions which the campaign would never attempt to counteract.

On Brian Lenihan the commentary stated:

Brian Lenihan was the best known candidate and the perceived front runner.

In overall terms, Brian Lenihan tends to be viewed as the best candidate for the job. He is widely liked and, for the most part, admired. He is thought of as friendly, outgoing, personable and extremely adept at the public relations aspects of his job. His recent illness evokes considerable sympathy but a substantial minority believe it is a mistake to have a man who they believe is seriously ill stand for a seven-year term as President.

Mr Lenihan is viewed as a very able politician but probably no more so than President Hillery before him. There is quite a widespread belief that he lacks depth. This is not a major disadvantage, given people's perceptions of the role of the Presidency at present. As we shall see in a moment, that role is already coming under question and one of the candidates, Mary Robinson, is seen to have taken a lead in making the re-definition of the role of the President an issue in the campaign.

Perhaps the greatest danger is of being seen as simply a continuation of the Hillery Presidency. More is expected than that. At this early stage in the campaign, the main threat comes from Mary Robinson. There is a danger of being seen as older, more settled, more allied to the low-key style of recent years and more inclined simply to react to events than to having a vision of the role of the Presidency in the future.

The analysis pinpointed with great accuracy the problems that Lenihan would encounter in the campaign, problems which the Party would never face up to. To do what the report was suggesting - present the candidate as a young, dynamic progressive - would have involved a major repackaging of Lenihan who was now far too old, far too settled, and "far too allied to the low-key style of recent years" to project what the research had so clearly shown the public wanted. In the end, the campaign simply ignored the advice, read the bits about Lenihan's popularity and ran him solely on that.

On Mary Robinson the commentary read:

Mary Robinson is seen as the dark horse of the election. She is a much more familiar figure in Dublin than outside. In Dublin she is widely recognised as the candidate for the Labour / Workers' Party. In provincial areas however her party affiliations are much less well-known.

Throughout the group discussions there was a surprisingly high level of awareness of the fact that she has introduced the role and functions of the President as an element in the debate. This is seen to be quite a healthy thing and she has been given considerable credit for it ... her progress will need to be watched with some care.

The fact that she is a woman draws considerable attention and the warmth of response to this notion (that of a female candidate) should not be underestimated. The feeling was expressed consistently throughout the group discussions that we are not yet ready for a female Taoiseach but the lesser demands of the Presidency mean that people are much more willing to accept the possibility of a female President.

Mary Robinson's stance on particular issues is reasonably well-known in Dublin and among middle class voters; less well-known in provincial areas or among those from working class backgrounds. Reactions to her appearance are positive - "She looks the part" - and is thought to have improved in recent times.

Her main areas of weakness are thought to be her stance on social issues, her lack of 'the common touch' and an association with Labour, and, more significantly, the Workers' Party. These problems are all more likely to be evident in provincial and rural areas than in Dublin where she has considerable strength and potential.

There is some recognition of the fact that she has attempted to distance herself from Labour and the Workers' Party. At one level this is seen as a strength - a move towards putting the Presidency above politics. The absence of any strong track record as a mainstream politician fits with this persona. On the negative side however, there is a recognition that something must be wrong if a candidate is stepping back from the people who provided her nomination.

The report was equally specific in relation to Austin Currie:

Austin Currie was regarded as a relatively recent nomination. There was widespread recognition that he was not the first choice of the Fine Gael Party and this is seen to be symptomatic of two elements:
* A disregard for the function of the Presidency within Fine Gael. This is linked by some people with their failure to nominate a candidate last time around and the treatment of President O'Dálaigh in the past.
* More widespread discontent within Fine Gael. It was suggested, for example, that Peter Barry did not run for the Presidency so that he could leave himself free to contest the leadership of the Party with Alan Dukes in the event that Fine Gael did badly in the Presidential Election.

At present Austin Currie is not seen as a strong candidate. In part, this derives from the fact that he is regarded as a substitute choice. More importantly, it derives from his northern Ireland origins and, most markedly, the fact that he has not 'served his time' to a sufficient degree since being elected to the Dáil.

There is always the possibility that he may become a more attractive candidate over time, particularly if he can convince people that he is stepping back from Party politics and bringing a broader 32-county dimension to the Presidential debate. For the moment however, he is seen as very much the outsider, in every sense of that word.

On more general issues the report concluded that the Presidency was not seen in very high regard, that it was "tame" and limited.

President Hillery is thought to have been a particularly low-key President. When asked to consider the topic, electors made much of the fact that they hardly ever see or hear anything about President Hillery; his functions or areas of involvement or special interest. There is a feeling that he was much more prominent in earlier roles, this perceived decline in impact tends to confirm people in their view that the role is very much a retiring one.

There is a strong feeling that the Taoiseach has taken on an increasingly Presidential style in recent years.

Armed with this information, with clear warnings about the Robinson impact and the need to project dynamism and change the Fianna Fáil campaign team swung into action.

The Party now knew they had to promote an 'active' Presidency. They also knew that Haughey, forever jealous of his own powers, would not tolerate any expansion of the Presidential role through Constitutional change. So Lenihan's speech at the launch of his campaign, scripted by the Taoiseach's own speech writer, Martin Mansergh, made a point of stating that any change in the Presidential role would be within the Constitutional parameters.

Sometime later, the other two candidates made similar qualifications to their vision of the Presidential role, but at that early stage, Lenihan's speech was seen as cautious, conservative, exactly the opposite impression the survey had urged the Party to portray.

In addition, the long recitation of his time in nine different administrations, the endless repetition of the fact that he had been more than a quarter of a century in active politics, conveyed less the idea of a widely experienced man than of one who must be so exhausted after such a lengthy career that he desperately needed a retirement job.

And Fianna Fáil did have one other handicap when it came to promoting a brand new active Presidency. By implication that meant that Hillery had been an unexciting passive President, a politically awkward comparison to make.

"The feeling that a Fianna Fáil President would provide more of the same kept being hammered home," said a campaign activist, "we knew that Hillery was a handicap but we couldn't hang him out to dry. The issue of how to make the Presidency interesting to the people was talked about a lot. Mary Robinson had already gone down that road offering the divil and all. She made outrageous claims early on but the controversy worked to her advantage ultimately. There was a clear perception that she was going to be different."

In the end, Fianna Fáil decided that the election was not about issues, that it would be an 'issueless' campaign.

"There wasn't a whole lot to market," said the same activist, "apart from Lenihan's qualities. We pushed the image of a family man, experienced, an international statesman."

The campaign slogan, 'The People's President' (as opposed to what?) was adopted, a slogan as bland and fatuous as the campaign itself. No attempt was made to promote ideas, vision, policies, to target particular groups, to appeal to particular electoral segments. Lenihan, like Currie, was simply pushed out and told to shake hands. The approach spoke volumes about the paucity of vision, imagination, direction and identity within Fianna Fáil itself.

As one activist put it: "Fianna Fáil is a catch-all Party, and it produces catch-all candidates. Was ours a bland campaign? Yes it was. We weren't trying to reach out in the way she was."

Apart from the spell of Lenihan's personality the Party was also confident of another buffer against defeat, that the fickle middle class, supposedly grateful for the improved national economic performance, "would not try" said one activist, "to destabilise the Government by upsetting Fianna Fáil." But research gradually detected that people clearly distinguished between Government satisfaction on the one hand and the election of a President on the other.

"In all the research Lenihan trailed the Party vote. That surprised us. We felt that he should have been much more comfortable in the polls."

Apart from the campaign team that met daily at Party HQ, another group had been set up by the Lenihan family, worried in view of the nomination saga, that the Party would not put its back into Lenihan's campaign. This group included Brian Lenihan junior, barrister Esmonde Smyth, and Frank Dunlop, a Public Relations consultant, who set up their own headquarters in Dunlop's Mount Street office just down the road from the Party HQ.

Smyth became the main speech writer, helped by friends in the Law Library and by Martin Mansergh. Six basic scripts were produced dealing with the international dimension of the Presidency, Lenihan's track record, and the promotion of an open and active Presidency.

The strategists had also identified a number of "soft non-controversial" areas that Lenihan could run with, principally the environment and sport.

But by and large the speeches were drivel, bland empty rhetoric that received little more than token coverage despite Mr Mara's attempts to get the news desks excited. News that Mr Lenihan would incorporate an Environment award in the President's annual *An Gaisce* awards failed to get anyone too worked up.

In one speech in Thurles on 10 October the Tánaiste took as his theme 'harmony', a word he then proceeded to mention no fewer than seven times. James Clarence Mangan was also quoted:

> *Oh Ireland be it thy high duty*
> *To teach the world the might of moral beauty*
> *And stamp God's image truly on the struggling soul.*

It was gruesome stuff, likely to appeal only to the more sentimental, maudlin elements of the electorate. In fairness, many of Currie's and Robinson's outpourings were also forgettable but Lenihan's scripts had a certain unique cringe factor.

"Look," said another key activist, "the general public, we felt, had no interest in the campaign. The biggest thing was Brian's popularity and there was no point in fighting it on policies. In a sense we had nothing to do except drive him round the country and pump out speeches which we knew were boring, totally boring. No one was seen as a serious threat and this led to apathy. We weren't getting the people out and because we wanted to avoid controversy Brian didn't want to attack the other candidates."

Throughout the early part of the campaign, accusations of an overly close relationship with the Taoiseach, and the effect this might have on a future Lenihan presidency were largely, and unwisely, ignored by the strategists.

"We made a mistake not trying to counterbalance that," said an activist. "We should have gone along the lines of 'loyalty equals trust' therefore 'disloyalty equals unreliability'. We should have said that Currie had been disloyal to the SDLP (by leaving them) and Robinson had flitted from constituency to constituency and had also walked out on the Labour Party. Why didn't we lash back? Because we didn't want to get into a mud fight. We had to keep the other candidates at their low level. Mixing it would bring them up and him down. Anyway at the beginning the accusation of blandness didn't really stick. The lack of excitement suited us because it was a lack of excitement with the whole campaign that affected the other candidates as well. We told RTE that they could interview Lenihan all they liked provided it was on a one to one basis. RTE wanted him on all the programmes but we said we didn't want to raise Currie and Robinson's profiles to Lenihan's level."

The campaign team also experienced difficulty in organising the national tour, pulled by the demands of the Lenihan family, by Brian himself, and by their own view of how things should be done.

Details of proposed itineraries had to be prepared days in advance and shown to Lenihan's wife Ann. For many in the campaign Mrs Lenihan was the most difficult element to deal with. She was understandably worried, constantly uptight about how much or how little people were doing for her husband, and would frequently publicly berate people as senior as Director of Elections and Minister for Labour Bertie Ahern. Lenihan's mood was frequently dictated by Ann Lenihan who tended to have a subduing effect on her husband.

Lenihan himself wanted to do a grand tour of every village and town, in the old style, while Ahern and others would have preferred just a handful of venues, but transformed into major events attracting more media attention. This problem was exacerbated by the fact that Mrs Lenihan wanted Brian home every night no matter where he was canvassing.

"We wanted to base the tour around the four Euro constituencies and have four major speeches," said a campaign member, "but in fact there was a different town and a different speech virtually every night. And Brian never wanted to deviate from the original six themes. So the whole thing got bogged down. The tour was so boring. We kept meeting the same kind of people, the same hard core activists and so it was really difficult to get him photographed with people other than the Party grassroots. All the local tour organisers wanted him photographed with them for when he became President so that they could stick it up on their mantelpieces and we ended up travelling to houses halfway up the sides of mountains just so they could get their picture taken. And then of course the Boss was opening his papers every day and seeing pictures of Currie and Robinson but none of Brian and he was throwing tantrums which didn't help anyone's morale."

The election broadcasts were also problematic. The original idea was to do a 'Life of Brian' style video but this was quickly ruled out because of the stark contrast between Lenihan, hale and healthy and fat in the face just a few years before, and the thin, gaunt man he had become during his illness.

The broadcasts that did go out were uninspired. Haughey himself featured in most of the first one, staring straight into the camera and talking about Lenihan's greatness. The second featured the candidate delivering his 'stump' speech over shots of the campaign and the third featured Brian and Ann in conversation after the tapes controversy. The poster campaign also ran into difficulties. Phase one featured billboard posters of Lenihan and his wife, Brian standing with one hand on her shoulder, an image, said one activist later, which looked like a typical Fianna Fáil male keeping the women down.

Phase two was designed to show Lenihan touring the country,

meeting with groups of people throughout the country. In the end, because of the tapes affair, those posters were never used. A different poster campaign was needed.

But the election apathy was not confined to the grassroots. There was plenty too at campaign team level, with many of those involved, convinced that Lenihan was a 'shoo in', simply going through the motions, getting out the posters, arranging the itinerary, writing the speeches, but with no attempt to actively counteract the Robinson appeal or to broaden Lenihan's.

Central to this was a type of Party paranoia, the fear from the top down that any attempt to strike out in a bold, imaginative way to snatch the elusive extra 4 to 6% would jeopardise the 44% core vote. It was conservatism and caution all the way.

"There was a great lethargy within the Party," said one TD, "on loads of occasions people simply didn't turn out to meet him. The feeling within the campaign team was that, Brian's a great guy, just let him at it. The underlying aim was to promote Brian as good old Brian, the sort of man you'd meet in the street and he'd talk to you and he'd probably say, sure don't I know your mother? We should have been more attuned to what was happening on the ground. I remember early on in the campaign meeting an old Fianna Fáil voter down the country, and he looked at me and he smiled and he said, Oh, I think I'll give the woman the stroke this time. But we didn't pick it up. Our feedback was faulty. People kept telling us that there was great turnout here, there and everywhere but none of us had been wherever it was and so we didn't know and of course Brian was always saying that things were grand. And of course people were trying to cover their own asses in the campaign, saying that the advertising was wonderful and this was wonderful and that was wonderful when it wasn't."

But whatever problems Fianna Fáil were having, they were as nothing compared to the ongoing agony in Fine Gael.

4

Ongoing Agony

As Senator Maurice Manning confided to Michael Noonan shortly after Austin Currie's nomination as the Fine Gael candidate, it was "a doomed exercise from the start."

With eight weeks to polling day, Director of Elections Jim Mitchell had on his hands a candidate that no sane party should have run, or at least not with just eight weeks to go.

Currie was, in the words of one campaign team member, "a Guinness Light candidate, someone that nothing was going to lift. They said it couldn't be done and they were right."

In addition Mitchell had a Party leader despised by the bulk of his Front Bench, a Party up to its neck in debt, apathetic backbenchers who had little intention of stirring themselves, and the certain though unspoken knowledge that the real Fine Gael candidate, as far as their own electorate was concerned, was a woman called Mary Robinson already playing a blinder in every godforsaken hamlet and urban centre in the country.

By the time Currie was selected, the Fine Gael mind had already settled on the idea of a two horse race. The stage was set for a nightmare campaign, one described much much later as "like a living death".

Three political forces were now at play in the election which Fine Gael were incapable of either counteracting or even spotting.

The first was that, despite the virtually unanimous consensus to the contrary, Lenihan was beatable. Early polls had shown that his appeal was limited to the core Fianna Fáil vote. A strong second-placed candidate could beat him on transfers.

The second force at play was that Robinson's Achilles Heel, 'the left-wing monkey on her back' had been skilfully neutralised by Bride Rosney and other sharp operators on her campaign team. It was the one issue on which Fine Gael could legitimately, in the eyes of their own supporters, attack her. Without that stick, they couldn't hope to successfully challenge her.

And the third force was the Fine Gael leadership issue. It underpinned and undermined the entire campaign. There was, as one campaign member said, a stench coming from Fine Gael, alienating their own supporters and effectively corrupting the whole course of the campaign. The issue dictated levels of morale within the party, acting as a distracting, chaos-inducing force in the campaign.

Not alone did Fine Gael have no vision of the Presidency as did Robinson, or any sense as to how a successful campaign could boost their own political agenda, as did Labour, there was a huge minority in the Party, who would rather not have fought it at all and who used the failure to select a candidate as a final excuse to oust the leader.

But that type of analysis was for the bars of Leinster House *after* the election. Meanwhile, Jim Mitchell had psyched himself up for the job ahead. In addition, he and his colleagues who would later move to depose Alan Dukes had quickly decided not to attempt to sabotage the election so as to ensure a Dukes defeat. They would work and furthermore they would be seen to work. They couldn't risk deflecting party anger at Dukes by conducting an apathetic, lack-lustre campaign.

Besides, they had seen the figures. Barring miracles, Currie was going nowhere from day one. He had bought Dukes some extra time but nothing could save the leader now. It would not destroy what one campaign team member described as "the hidden agenda" of the Currie election to go all out to work for him.

The formulation of a policy, an image for Currie and the type of Presidency he would project was a tortuous affair. Currie was insistent that the idea of an open active Presidency should be pursued, if only to draw down differences between what could be and what had been witnessed in the fourteen years of Paddy Hillery's term in office. Party research had also shown a desire amongst the public for changes in the presidential role. Currie's image was to be that of a young family man, oozing integrity and vigour.

The draft document of *A New Style of Presidency* was originally drawn up by Jim Mitchell and barrister Peter Shanley. In late September Shanley had researched the legal parameters of the President's role, what she or he was or wasn't constitutionally empowered to do. Mitchell then revised it, producing a document which he felt was "impactful and well written."

Alan Dukes had other ideas. He received the document the night before the Front Bench was due to meet to approve it. Dukes in effect vetoed the document, producing the following morning his own document which Mitchell in turn thought useless.

In the end a mish mash of the two was drafted although drawing more on Mitchell's ideas than on Dukes's. The result, distributed to the media, was impressive looking, but largely ignored by the media. It was full of good, worthy ideas about the Presidency which never took off because Currie himself never did.

The strategy was to concentrate on a new issue every week. In the end, the campaign became so bogged down on northern Ireland and later, the tapes controversy, that six major speeches were left to gather dust on the shelves. Currie's proposals, some of which may have been constitutionally questionable included the President making an annual address to the Dáil and Seanad, chairing an Overseas Aid Development Commission, chairing a permanent Judicial Commission, chairing an Environment Council, chairing a National Sports and Recreation Council and setting up a Presidential Merit Awards Scheme.

In themselves they were good ideas. But what Currie and his team failed to do was to thread their campaign with a single linking theme as Robinson did. In the end, Currie was simply pushed around the length and breadth of the country making worthy speeches about commissions and emigrants, but failing to impinge on the public consciousness.

*

In the end, all three candidates promoted the same basic theme - An Open Presidency. Many of their speeches were indistinguishable, making the same general statements about promoting Ireland, giving minority groups recognition, making the Office and the Aras more accessible.

But Currie's problem was credibility. All the ideas, however boring and fatuous, at least sounded plausible coming from Robinson and Lenihan. Both had been around the southern Irish political scene for a long time, were familiar with its institutions and were perceived as knowing what they were talking about.

How could Currie, a resident in the south for little more than year speak with credibility and in detail about an Office which few people imagined he really knew about?

The President is perceived as someone with a wide knowledge of and familiarity with every aspect of Irish life. On that score Currie in the public mind simply wasn't at the races.

Currie's outsider status was graphically highlighted by a Currie 'own goal' - he alone of the candidates couldn't even cast his vote on election day, he wasn't registered. Instead he went to a local polling booth to shake hands with people there in order to let RTE do their customary election day picture. In fact what had happened could equally have happened to anyone - he had moved house in his constituency and had failed to register. But the image of the voteless Currie undoubtedly cemented the outsider image.

Mitchell's first task was to put in place an election organisation. The labyrinthine - or Byzantine as one activist called it - structure that emerged arose from Mitchell's mistaken belief that as many people as possible had to be given a role, a title, in order to motivate them.

The organisational structure was both gargantuan and tortuous. Drawn up on an A4 sheet it looked like a complex family tree with bundles of obscure distant cousins clinging on to the outer limbs. It might have worked in a less pressurised, longer campaign but in the brief desperate race that was the Currie campaign, what was needed was a tight, internal structure with centralised authority and no more than two or three people making decisions.

In all there were eighteen people on the national campaign committee headed up by Jim Mitchell and his deputy Peter Shanley plus a total of twenty-two more on various regional, finance, publicity and tour committees. While, on paper, everyone had a distinct separate role to play, in reality the whole structure merged into one with constant overlapping of roles and authority and vital energy wasted on sorting out the pecking order.

Reflecting with hindsight on the campaign structure and on the campaign generally, it is difficult for those involved to keep a note of hysteria out of their voices.

Austin Currie had not one but two personal assistants -

Maurice Manning representing the Parliamentary Party and Brian Brady from Dublin West.

In addition to Brian Brady who was keeping tabs on Currie for the sake of the constituency, John Bruton also had a function there as Dublin West special director. He in turn had two more people helping him, Mary Banotti MEP and former Fine Gael TD George Birmingham.

Alan Dukes also had a minder, with Gay Mitchell appointed as his Personal Assistant. Again, no one really knew what exactly Mitchell was supposed to do.

Dublin South West, with no sitting Fine Gael TD, was honoured by not one, but two special directors, Senator Avril Doyle and Charlie Flanagan, a Laois-Offaly TD, Doyle having another role as assistant to Mitchell on the campaign Committee.

"It was cumbersome, illogical," said one member of the campaign team, "with invented jobs. There were forty-eight people in all with Important and Central positions and everyone thinking that because of their fancy title they had the right to make decisions. Our energy was dissipated just in struggling with the internal organisation. We were constantly looking inwards instead of outwards with endless meetings and meetings about meetings. We had a national strategy committee meeting every Thursday for the fist few weeks but this was abandoned because it was too big and after that it wasn't really replaced. Mitchell took to meeting with *ad hoc* groups rather than with a core group so no one really knew what was going on or who was making the decisions. Dozens of people had to be informed about even the most trivial decision. I mean even buying a tie for Austin say, Currie's personal minder Brian Brady had to be consulted as well as Currie's parliamentary personal assistant Maurice Manning. That may be a bit exaggerated but it's not too far off the truth." "In previous elections," said a party official, "we had our planning and strategy done way in advance and everything just fell into place. In this election that wasn't done. It was chaos. Every bloody parliamentarian had a job. The whole thing was a massive endurance test. New people kept being dragged in whenever anything went wrong. It was eight weeks of mania. It was the limits of human tolerance."

In this morass it was difficult for anyone to pinpoint a clear direction. Madeleine Taylor-Quinn, organising the national tour, could be given one direction by one campaign member, countermanded by another member and would then receive even more advice from an associate down in her own constituency.

The Curries themselves appeared confused by the whole campaign. In Tyrone, they were used to running a small, tight-knit campaign team, headed by Annita Currie and staffed by Austin's brothers and family members. Here the structure was beyond their grasp with Currie constantly having to look over his shoulder to make sure that plans which he wouldn't accept were not being cooked up by Mitchell and the boys behind his back. It was, for the Tyrone man, a sharp culture shock.

In addition Currie had expected something quite different, at the very least more professional, from the experienced men and women on the team. He had imagined a core group planning strategy, issues, polling continuously to see what people were interested in, doing advance planning in terms of TV and radio programmes. He saw little evidence of any of this.

The element of professionalism he had expected simply wasn't there. Because of the lack of time he saw his role in terms of pressing the flesh and talking to the media. He also had to enthuse the workers. As far as he was concerned that was his job. The strategic end of it was a matter for headquarters,

The way he should present the campaign themes was also a matter for them. He expected people to come to him, "well there's a theme here, we have taken opinion polls and have been advised by our marketing people that there's a theme here that ought to be developed." But it didn't happen.

Currie had been watching too many movies ...

Jim Mitchell's role as Director of Elections was widely seen as honourable, but flawed. For Mitchell, for the reasons outlined above, had been handed a virtually impossible task. He worked, say his campaign colleagues, like a demon, a ball of energy forever calling and attending meetings, thinking up scams, issuing statements, but with little result. He was a terrific constituency organiser and a superb vote manager but he lacked the breadth to conduct a truly national campaign.

And it was Mitchell who was also blamed for two of the biggest mistakes Fine Gael made in the campaign - the public, boastful, claim that the *Questions and Answers* Lenihan tapes programme was a trap even though, at the time, there was no evidence that it was anything other than a set of happy coincidences, and his statement to reporters that Currie would come last, several days before polling.

The 'trap' claim incensed Fine Gael voters the length and breadth of the country. They phoned Party headquarters and local TDs accusing the Party of using dirty 'Fianna Fáil type' tactics. And Mitchell was left in no doubt about the level of Currie's anger.

Watching newspaper coverage of his campaign convinced Currie that the strategy team, his backup, were not doing their job. His best 'picture opportunity', a photograph of himself and John B Keane at the premiere of *The Field*, was arranged not by HQ but by Currie himself and Kerry North TD Jimmy Deenihan, a close friend of Keane's. In addition, he felt that some picture and report coverage was blatantly biased towards Robinson.

Again, unlike the Robinson campaign, Fine Gael failed to target any particular segments of the electorate that Currie should make a point of canvassing.

Robinson had targeted active, caring groups, doing great work, showing great spirit to whom, she said, she could give a voice. In that sense her national tour was not aimless but very deliberately targeted at a group outside her own natural constituency to whom she could deliver an attractive message. Currie was simply told to shake hands with Ireland.

Austin Currie also felt that his wife Annita, a teacher, and involved with handicapped children could, if let, do an effective job of neutralising some of Robinson's appeal to the marginalised and to women by doing her own canvass of community and other groups. She had taken two months off her job to help out. Yet throughout the campaign, the Curries never felt that Annita was used to best advantage.

But the logistics of the campaign did fall into place, the surface details which the Party could execute on automatic pilot. Hoardings and bus sides were booked, campaign photographs taken, leaflets distributed.

The advertising agency, DDFH&B Limited, was asked to produce campaign posters and hoardings which would evoke a new style of Presidency. They took the instruction literally, producing the campaign slogan *A New Style of Presidency*. "The advertising was good," one campaign member said, "but it backed up an ineffectual candidate."

Photographs, advertising, all were high quality but inside the campaign was a vacuum which no one had either the time, energy or imagination to fill. Fine Gael had no strategy for selling the message, no specific interest groups targeted. It was simply rhetoric stitched onto an aimless national tour - and a tour which showed the Curries just who was on Dukes's side and who wasn't. In anti-Dukes constituencies, the TDs on the ground did the bare minimum of postering and canvassing. Later, when HQ would phone individual constituencies looking for canvass reports, there were none.

The national tour, organised by a four-person committee headed by Clare TD Madeleine Taylor-Quinn was widely criticised - an old-fashioned 'shaking hands with everyone model' which the Party had ditched, or thought they had ditched, years ago.

"Currie was trying to shake 2.4 million hands," said a Party official, "and that just isn't on any more. There's no point in going to every bloody little crossroads and hamlet in the country if the only people who are going to see you at that crossroads are three oul fellas and a cow. You need to stage big events with lots of people in selected places and then make sure that they're televised. We did not have 'Mary Robinson time' to go around massaging every little village."

In addition changes were constantly made in the itinerary with no one sure who had made them or why. "We wondered sometimes," said an activist "whether a change was a typographical error or genuine."

*

The first three weeks of the campaign did go well - a lightning tour of the constituencies to meet activists who had never clapped eyes on Currie before and were badly in need of motivation - and to meet the editors of regional newspapers. By the end of three weeks Currie had got widespread, local coverage in virtually every provincial paper and radio station and had apparently gone down very well with the activists.

So to prove to themselves that what they were witnessing on the ground was an accurate reflection of the electorate's real feelings about Currie, Fine Gael did their own poll of the Dublin area towards the end of September.

The news was heartening. In three weeks he had risen from a low of 15% to 24% in Dublin. But at the same time MRBI were also conducting a national poll for the party. On Saturday 29 September, Fine Gael's poll results came through. Two days later, Monday 1 October the MRBI national poll came through.

MRBI gave them the Dublin results first. They confirmed the trend the party had picked up in their own poll - a 7% increase in the Dublin vote. The initial surge of activity appeared to have paid off.

Excitement mounted - the first glimmer of hope in the campaign to date. But the other results were devastating. The trend in the country was the reverse. Fine Gael's vote among the farmers had collapsed - from 40% to 20% In other words, the Party itself was getting 40% from the farmers but Currie was picking up just half that Party vote. Currie was simply a massive turn-off for one of the most crucial sectors of the Fine Gael vote, despite the candidate's rural background.

And the problem with the farmers would never be overcome despite an endorsement later in the election from Mark Clinton for 'Farmer' Currie. And the result of that late September poll, which Currie was never shown, matched the vote he actually received at the ballot boxes less than six weeks later - 17%. Subsequently the Dublin vote itself would recede and, after the tapes controversy, the man was effectively abandoned as the election became a battle between just two candidates.

But that was still some time off. In the meantime Jim Mitchell and his campaign team set to tackling the issue which they believed was fundamental to Currie's problems - northern Ireland.

Ignored in the early stages, the team eventually realised they simply couldn't duck it - they would have to make a virtue out of it, persuade Currie to put his name to some headline-grabbing initiative on the issue and then bury it and get on with rest of the campaign. It was this plan that led to one of the most intractable problems of the campaign, exposing tensions between Currie and his campaign handlers and getting the campaign so bogged down that other initiatives had to be shelved.

The tension arose between the campaign team's desire to

create controversy and rustle up some much-needed interest in their campaign, and Currie's deep-seated reluctance to trivialise either his life and career in the north or to lower himself in the eyes of his former colleagues by striking new poses or taking up positions other than those he had espoused all his life.

Despite casting himself upon the bosom of the Fine Gael party Currie had never cut the northern political umbilical cord. If he had one thing, and only one thing, going for him in the eyes of the people of the south, it was his integrity on the northern issue. He would not ditch that now, no matter what - an attitude which met with near derision from elements in the campaign.

"We just couldn't get Currie to say anything new about the north," said one prominent campaign member. "I came to realise that the 'not-an-inch' policy wasn't just a Unionist thing. There was this incredible caution, incredible reluctance to move, to think of fresh things, anything that would in any way be new, novel, daring, out of kilter with the SDLP. We kept saying we wanted something dramatic, we really struggled with him."

A communications group under Michael Noonan had been set up, responsible for speeches, media interviews and other publicity. Apart from TDs the group also included Shane Molloy, marketing manager of Lever brothers and Mark Mortell, of the Ballygowan group. Also on the group was Brian Lynch of the *Irish Press*, a personal friend of Alan Dukes, nominated to the team by Dukes.

A special meeting to tackle the northern issue was convened. Mitchell told the group that the ongoing 'talks about talks' process initiated by the northern Ireland Secretary of State, Peter Brooke, was going nowhere. The whole thing, in Mitchell's words was "a pain in the face". The SDLP, said Mitchell, had been talking about a referendum of all the people of Ireland in the event of a new agreement being put forward if the Brooke initiative did succeed. Why not, said Mitchell, have a referendum before the event, to state the formal position of the 26 Counties that there would be no unity without the consent of the northern majority, why not have a 'peace' referendum which would modify Articles 2 and 3? In other words, a referendum to effectively neutralise the political force of the territorial claim over northern Ireland by inserting into the Constitution the northern Unionist consent clause. Such a move would go beyond stated Fine Gael policy and would not accord with SDLP policy either.

Currie wasn't present at the meeting which appeared to welcome Mitchell's plan. Brian Lynch was asked to come up with a script and within twenty-four hours had done so.

The following morning Dukes called Mitchell and Noonan into his office. Lynch's script was already on his desk even though the meeting that launched it hadn't ended until 10pm the previous night. Mitchell thought the speech was tremendous, powerful, the best script he'd seen for a long time.

Lynch had suggested that Currie would propose a referendum to allow the Irish people to say categorically that there would be no unity without consent, and that the Irish Government would not get involved in any talks with the northern parties in relation to a new agreement in the north until the referendum had been approved. And because any referendum would necessitate the Dáil passing a special Bill this would open up a 'natural' gap in normal Anglo-Irish business which would allow the Unionists the opportunity to engage in dialogue with other northern parties and with the British Government, something they had been steadfastly refusing to do until the Anglo-Irish Agreement was suspended.

But Currie wouldn't have it. The speech and its apparent widespread acceptance within the communications group betrayed a lack of sensitivity about his position. He was deeply angered at the scheme, telling Mitchell and others that if the election depended of him taking all this stuff on board then he had had enough of it.

Currie simply wouldn't wear the referendum or more precisely the idea of no Irish involvement in talks until it had got through. He knew the whole idea would either delay talks on the north or present an excuse to the Unionists to further drag their feet because of the timescale involved. The team told him not to worry, there was damn all chance of getting the referendum Bill through the Dáil in the first place. They simply wanted him to mouth the rhetoric, put forward the idea. He didn't have to worry about follow-through because there would be none. It was of course a deeply cynical exercise but - needs must.

The two sides battled it out for a fortnight, time and energy wasted with the election date now in their sights. His first reaction was to say leave it with me, returning later with his open text, leaving in the idea of a referendum but insisting that it would not take place until *after* the successful conclusion of talks.

Mitchell felt the text was completely watered down, without impact, a routine restatement of well-known positions on the Anglo-Irish process. He was now desperate for Currie to make some impact. He needed some controversy, any controversy, positive controversy, to make the man relevant to the campaign, to make people want to say YES! In the end Mitchell forced Currie to redraft his statement, with Currie doing so only after he had consulted SDLP colleagues in Monaghan the night before the initiative was finally launched, and with Unionist MP Ken McGuinness.

Then came the idea, never seriously put to Currie because half the communications group balked at it, for Currie to put the northern problem in the context of the ancient enmity between the islands of Ireland and of Great Britain, to show that the Unionist problem was only a more recent manifestation of the core one, that the country should begin to dwell on the old problem and seek to remedy it by building up a new relationship between the two countries. To that effect, Currie would say in a speech that he hoped that the day would come when he as President could invite the Queen of England quite happily to stay with him in Aras an Uachtaráin. Positive controversy.

Half the group said fantastic, the other half buried their heads in their hands. When Currie heard about it he said, po-faced, that since he was young enough to serve two terms as President he might consider it in his second. Another plan was for Currie to visit the Republican prisoners in Portlaoise prison and issue a statement there lamenting the waste of young lives and hoping that in a fresh new Ireland circumstance would no longer permit young men to turn to taking up arms in the name of the Republic. However, it was swiftly pointed out that this line neatly dovetailed with that of the Provos, that it was political circumstances that had landed these men in jail and nothing else. That idea too was swiftly abandoned.

In the end a special press conference was convened, in the Constitution Room of the Shelbourne Hotel, to launch the watered down non-controversial peace pledge and referendum initiative.

By now Currie had had his spot on RTE's *Today Tonight* and those on the campaign team felt he had lost an opportunity to get ahead.

Currie proposed that all three candidates would sign a peace pledge which would then form the basis for a peace referendum "at the earliest possible opportunity". The pledge would express the will of the people of the state that unity would come about only with the agreement of a majority of people in the north. It would also state that the use of violence for political ends is contrary to the will of the people.

At the press conference one journalist commented that the whole thing was rather like pledging that one was against sin. Pressed again and again to state clearly and categorically that he wanted to see the modification of Articles 2 and 3 of the Constitution, Currie resolutely refused to say so, stating only that any future agreement would be likely to have implications for the Constitution.

The whole thing, as Mitchell had predicted, was a damp squib, largely ignored by the other two candidates. It was dutifully reported in the press and then forgotten. It was now 18 October, less than three weeks to polling day. One third of the official campaign had been taken up with an issue which did absolutely nothing for Currie's prospects. It was, said one, the most significant thing he did during the whole campaign, but not nearly as significant as he had wanted it to be.

Everything else of a controversial nature which was subsequently put to Currie was also turned down. Mitchell constantly nagged him, telling him, look we're ironing everything out, there's no controversy, no nothing, we're never going to lift this campaign. Currie also refused to do a *Hot Press* interview, much to Mitchell's disgust.

*

And then came Mitchell's only window of opportunity - Mary Robinson's own apparently damning *Hot Press* interview, which is treated in detail elsewhere in this book. During the course of it Robinson had outlined trenchant views on a number of controversial topics, including homosexuality and family planning. She had also stated that as President, she would be able to look Charlie Haughey in the eye and tell him to back off. She also said that "the whole patriarchal male dominated presence of the Church is probably the worst aspect of all the establishment forces that have sought to do down women over the years."

But her most controversial statement, and one which could have gutted her, if the media hadn't decided to back off or if the timing of a favourable opinion poll published a few days later had not been misunderstood in the press, was her apparent assent to the opening of an illegal contraceptive stall.

Asked if she would perform the official launch of a contraceptive store in the Virgin Megastore (which had just been prosecuted for selling condoms illegally) Robinson's reply was:

> Yes. This is a very young country and I think it would be helpful to have a President that would be in touch with what young people are doing.

As is customary in *Hot Press* when they realise they have a controversial interview on their hands, some of the juicier extracts were faxed to the national papers and to RTE. *Hot Press* has a relatively small circulation, but coverage in the national papers would increase sales spectacularly.

The papers flagged the interview on the morning it hit the streets, noting in particular the Virgin Megastore reference and other more colourful extracts. Robinson then went on the *News at One* to explain herself, thereby getting herself further in the manure.

Asked by the interviewer about officiating at the opening of a contraceptive stall Mary Robinson answered.

> Yes, I have the text of the interview. I did not say yes at the start of that question ... what I was saying in answer to the trendy way the question was being put is that I would like to be in touch with young people and with the issues of concern to young people. certainly I am misquoted there or the reporter misunderstood what I said.

In a later interview, Mary Robinson, forced to acknowledge that she actually had said yes, described it as "a mannerism".

Mitchell well knew this pointed to trouble for Mary Robinson and a chance for Currie to catch up.

Earlier that week, on 1 October, the results of the first MRBI poll for Fine Gael had come through, showing Currie trailing at 17%. The mood of the campaign team was low and, at a meeting to discuss the *Hot Press* interview on 4 October, they knew that "Currie has to get in on this."

A call was put through to RTE and it was arranged that Currie would go on the *Six One* news to discuss it. Currie was spending the day canvassing north Dublin shopping centres with Mary Banotti and Richard Bruton.

"We wanted him to come in and sock it to Mary Robinson," said one team member, "in the sense that he'd come in and damn her with faint praise. He'd say that the woman was entitled to her views, why was there such controversy, sure she was *well known* for these views." In other words, Currie wouldn't criticise her views on controversial subjects *per se*, simply bring them once again to everyone's attention and try to damage her that way.

Press Officer Peter White had set the whole thing up. The *Six One* slot was secured, the statement was typed and waiting for Currie when he got back to campaign headquarters.

But he refused. The statement had been read to Currie on a car telephone line, Currie now on his way to Swords. The scrupulously cautious Currie refused to agree to any statement until he had a copy in his hands. Curie had come from a political culture where statements made were never casual, where every nuance was teased out for possible damaging even lethal impact. That caution he had never shrugged off. HQ agreed to fax it on to an office in Swords.

Once in Swords Currie read the full statement. He didn't like it. Even if he had agreed with its sentiments he was still in two minds whether Fine Gael should be in the business of attacking Mary Robinson in the first place. At the back of his mind was a future vote transfer deal and any vote transfer would have to be credible. If a situation now developed where Currie and Robinson were scoring points off each other, would a transfer pact be credible? Currie at this stage still thought he could finish second.

But Currie was also taking an even longer term view. If he didn't win the Presidency and did badly, he didn't want to be pilloried for having lost it by making stupid or controversial statements. The bottom line was that he didn't want to jeopardise his post-election career by giving in to the hysteria of the moment, even if it did give him a fillip in the polls.

And if Mary Robinson had to be attacked, which she had to be in some way to gain ground, were these the right issues to attack her on?

Currie then began to draft a statement of his own, sitting in the rehabilitation centre in Swords. He attacked her, not on the Catholic Church remarks and other issues which HQ had included in their statement but on her statements about forcing a sitting Taoiseach to "back off." This was questionable constitutional territory, a lack of responsibility, but it was not the 'sexy' attack issue Mitchell wanted him to go on. It would not remind the conservative wedge of the electorate of the controversial social issues Robinson championed.

But by the time he got to HQ, owing to unfortunately heavy traffic, it was too late to leg it to RTE in any case. But even if he had been on time, Currie still had no intention of going on.

"We had a speech, a statement," said one activist, "all agreed by the experts but he wouldn't do it. He just wouldn't do anything controversial. He kept saying he'd have to have time to consider. We kept trying to say to him, because we were all used to national elections, that you have to react quickly to things or else the whole thing is past. So he wouldn't go, and at half an hour's notice we wheeled Garret in. We had a couple of scripts in reserve and Garret used his script on the fact that she wasn't sound on the Anglo-Irish Agreement and neither was Lenihan. Garret was very good to us even though he was rather uneasy about it."

Mitchell and others felt, correctly, that the issue would be allowed die if the momentum wasn't kept up. Fianna Fáil's strategy at the time was not to allow Lenihan 'mix it' with the other candidates for fear of heightening their profiles and, apart from private glee at Robinson's gaffe, they did little to keep the pot boiling.

"Our belief was that if we did this right, that Currie would have been launched right into the thing and that the real debate would have started and that we really would have seized the opportunity. The problem was that that article never really penetrated the public consciousness ... it takes repetition, controversy to impinge on public consciousness ... we had wanted Currie to get in and engage her in debate - to hammer her."

But Currie still refused. The following day a reluctant John Bruton issued a statement taking Robinson to task for the divisiveness of some of the views she had expressed. But the Party's heart wasn't in it. How could they attack a woman who was not only popular with an unfortunate majority of their own supporters but whose views on so many social matters mirrored their own?

"It wasn't that we disagreed with her, but she gave us an opportunity and in any match or game or battle, you seize your opportunities as they arise without having scruples about whether you agree with certain things or not."

It was a no-win situation for Fine Gael. They knew the battle was with Robinson. They had to come second but could do so only by attacking and getting ahead of her. But attacking her made the Party feel deeply uncomfortable. The only attack issue which received the approval of a majority in the party was the Workers' Party, 'reds under the bed' smear they launched towards the end.

Currie's eventual statement on the *Hot Press* issue came at last on 8 October, the same day as the first *Irish Times* MRBI opinion poll showing him trailing with a dismal 19%, with Robinson now streaking ahead with 32% and Lenihan still riding high with 49% and more than four days after the *Hot Press* issue had hit the streets. It was half-hearted, with Currie pulling his punches right through.

> ... Mrs Robinson in her *Hot Press* article and the subsequent confusion of several interviews has played into the hands of Fianna Fáil. We can all make mistakes and Mrs Robinson can be forgiven for making her mistake. But she should not allow herself to be pushed by the extreme fringes of the left-wing beyond sound legal judgement. I would now suggest to Mrs Robinson that she would deprive Fianna Fáil of propaganda against expanding the Presidency by unreservedly withdrawing those statements in her interview which are unconstitutional, or illegal or divisive.

Currie in fact saw the lack of controversy in his campaign as a badge of honour, repeatedly saying that he was the only one who had made no mistakes. Mitchell's view was that the man who makes no mistakes makes nothing. Even subsequent good performances on RTE's *Today Tonight* and the *Late Late Show* were publicly applauded by the election team but privately derided.

"If he was that good on television, why then did he not register on some votes. Who decides he was very good? It's like saying a soap powder ad is very good - but you don't buy it."

By now the core campaign group knew that the situation was hopeless. "The atmosphere was awful," said one activist. "It was like a living death. I hated going to Front Bench meetings and Parliamentary Party meetings. There was no point in it, no purpose. Currie had been pushed out and told to perform and that was it. There was a touch of the surreal to the whole thing. You had all these strong speeches about how we were going to do in the face of the most awful poll results. Dukes could give no direction because of his position. It was heavy-handed, with sporadic involvement. He had no real ideas, he was a sad figure during it, ragged."

And whatever about the Electorate, Mitchell and the others had enormous difficulties in getting their own TDs and Senators on side.

"One third of the party," said one TD, "the liberal one third, were strongly for her and anyway didn't see him as a Fine Gael candidate at all - she was more their type; the conservative one third of the party, the Cosgrave wing, and the Johnny Boland wing, didn't associate him as a Party candidate and felt that a vote for him would be just an encouragement for Dukes to stay on. So we really had one third trying to carry the show."

It became increasingly impossible, because of strong resistance from the liberal wing in Fine Gael to attack Robinson. If they didn't they had little hope of catching up, if they did, the party would emerge from the election more deeply divided than ever.

We had a terrible problem because the liberal wing, in their hearts were really with Mary, they identified with her, not only in the Parliamentary Party but in the Party at large. She stood for the more open, progressive Party that people joined Fine Gael for. It had been Garret's view that the Party should move in that direction. So there was nothing we could do about it. We had a particular problem with the women TDs, women members generally, Senators and so on. We wanted a statement of endorsement from them for Austin and we convened them together in Dukes's office and they came in and they wriggled and they wouldn't issue a statement. Nuala Fennell proposed that they be left to draft a statement themselves and then come back. So we saw the difficulty and let them. So they went off, had a meeting then came back but there was no statement.

So Currie never got a national statement of endorsement from the women of his party. They simply wouldn't do it. Some, like Madeleine Taylor-Quinn and Avril Doyle did support the ideas but the more liberal feminists amongst the women, Nuala Fennell and Monica Barnes, Nora Owen and Mary Banotti, were the most reluctant (although Barnes and Fennell did appear in a party political broadcast). It wasn't that they didn't like or support Austin, they did and they worked for him but they just couldn't give him a public endorsement on behalf of women, when all their hopes, and beliefs were being carried by the candidacy of Mary Robinson.

Reflecting on the campaign in the end, one key activist said, "What we had was worse than no strategy. We had conflicting strategies. Our first strategy was that we were going to win on Mary Robinson's transfers which was ludicrous. Our second strategy was that we're going to come second but to do that we have to attack Mary Robinson and to do that we have to brand her a commie. So we do. Then our third strategy is that we're going to come third but we can't let Lenihan win so we better stop calling her a commie. Fast. From the very beginning, from the selection of a candidate to the end, we simply didn't face reality".

5
Mature Recollection

In 1986 King Juan Carlos of Spain paid a state visit to Ireland, his visit coinciding with a quest by a young University College Dublin (UCD) undergraduate for a suitable subject for his second year BA project in Politics.

By chance, the student, Navan-born Jim Duffy, tuned into radio coverage of the visit and, discussing the visit later with a college lecturer, hit upon the idea of doing his project on the role of the European Monarchy.

In his third year he had to choose a domestic political topic, and given that he now had extensive knowledge of other European Heads of State, he decided to tackle the Irish Presidency.

The project fascinated him. Fellow academics were also fascinated, avid to know his sources. So little was known about the nature of the office by academics and politicians alike, that Duffy knew he had discovered uncharted territory. The decision some time later to expand his BA project into his MA thesis topic was an obvious one.

Duffy's political contacts were good, particularly in Fine Gael. He had joined the UCD branch of Young Fine Gael in 1984 "dragged along by my best friend." He became an active member of the officer board and was later "talked into going for the Chairmanship" in 1986. He served until 1987. Stepping down, he says, he ceased to have an active role and drifted away.

But his brief foray into active politics had yielded powerful contacts including former Taoiseach Garret Fitzgerald and his own constituency TD, John Bruton, interviewed for his third year thesis. He had also made friends with young Fianna Fáil members in the college, people who would play a crucial role in events that would unfold more than three years later.

Duffy also had another political acquaintance - a young man called Brian Murphy, Chairperson of Young Fine Gael after Duffy in 1987, an individual so well got with the party hierarchy that it would be he who would be chosen on 22 October to sit in the audience to put searching questions to Brian Lenihan on that night's *Questions and Answers* programme on RTE.

But all of that was in the future. Duffy began his thesis. Politicians, he had decided, would be his primary source. He did not want to rely on archival material but rather to create his own theoretical framework as to how the office functioned and how other politicians viewed the office. Unravelling the events of the night of 27 January 1982, would, Duffy felt, be critical to this.

That night the Fine Gael-Labour Coalition Government had been defeated on a budget vote shortly after 8:00pm. The then Taoiseach Garret Fitzgerald announced that he would immediately go to Aras an Uachtaráin to request President Hillery to dissolve the Dáil.

In fact Fitzgerald didn't go to the Aras until 10:00pm and in the meantime Fianna Fáil engaged in frantic efforts to see if they could form a Government without a General Election. Party leader Charlie Haughey spoke to Independent TD Neil Blaney, seeking his support and also to Kildare TD Charlie McCreevy who had been expelled from the Fianna Fáil Parliamentary Party a short time earlier for moving against the Party leader.

In a later newspaper interview a spokesperson for Neil Blaney stated that at that meeting Mr Blaney had discussed with Mr Haughey the fact that the President had a right under the Constitution to call in the leader of the Opposition and attempt to form an alternative Government.

According to *The Sunday Press* report "[the] leader of the Opposition was quite amenable to Mr Blaney's proposals even to the extent of forming a National Government for six months."

The author has also learned that Mr Haughey told McCreevy at their meeting that attempts were being made to contact the President to ask him not to dissolve the Dáil but to call on Haughey instead to form a Government.

Earlier, at 8.25pm, Fianna Fáil had issued a statement saying that Haughey was available for consultation with the President should he so wish.

In the years that followed several accounts of the events of that night were written. It was claimed that phone calls had been made that night to the Aras, that none had got through, and that the calls had been made by Haughey, Brian Lenihan and former Fianna Fáil TD and Minister, Sylvester Barrett.

Apart from knowing of these accounts, Jim Duffy says that he had also spoken to senior civil servants, and to a source who had spoken to Brian Lenihan about the phone calls allegations and who had not received a denial.

He now felt certain that Lenihan and others had placed phone calls to Aras an Uachtaráin that night. What was also taken as fact was that not one of the callers had spoken to President Hillery directly.

Why were the events of that night so crucial to his thesis? Because, he has said, it showed the extent to which the President has powers that are not fully understood by politicians, and the extent to which politicians would like to push the President to do certain things if it was in their own interests. The incident also outlined the relationship between a President and his former party.

Duffy's letter to Brian Lenihan requesting an interview was sent in early May 1990. It read:

Dear Tánaiste,

I am at present researching the office of President of Ireland for my Master of Arts thesis in political science. I have decided, in my approach to the subject to examine, not just the powers and role of the President, but the perception of the presidential office possessed both by past holders of the office and by senior politicians. It is in this regard that I am writing to you.

Given your length of service in Government, your recollections of past Presidents, and in particular your general observations on the presidential office, would be of immense value to my research. In view of this, would it be possible for me to interview you?

My principal areas of interest would include the following:

1   The nature of the relationship between the Taoiseach and President (eg the constitutional duty of the Taoiseach to brief the President, etc)

2   The different approaches to office of successive Irish Presidents

3   The Presidency as viewed from Leinster House during your period in the Oireachtas

4   Specific incidents involving the Presidency (eg the allegation that President de Valera convinced Kevin

Boland not to resign in 1969, de Valera's support for Jack Lynch during the Arms Crisis, the Donegan-O'Dálaigh incident and the events surrounding the collapse of the first Fitzgerald coalition in January 1982, etc)

As I have said, your help on any or all of the above would be of immense value to me in my research. I have provisionally planned to have my thesis completed by mid-June. As such, should you be available, could I arrange to interview you at some stage between now and the end of May?

I look forward to receiving your reply.

Lenihan responded with alacrity, directing his personal secretary Brian Spain to contact Duffy and set up an interview. A call to Duffy's flat from Spain came through within a fortnight of posting the letter. There was no problem, said Spain, Brian will meet you on the 17 May - and he'll talk about everything apart from the current election. And by the way, said a laughing Spain, as he rang off, Brian is delighted that someone is researching the Presidency ...

Duffy arrived, late, to Leinster House, shortly after lunchtime on 17 May. Shown into Lenihan's office his first reaction was one of visible shock at Lenihan's appearance. He looked ghastly.

Then it was Lenihan's turn to look alarmed as he noted Duffy's expression. He rushed to reassure him. I'm OK, he said, I'm not dying, don't worry. The medicine I'm on, he added, makes me look drawn. A few days ago, he added, he had slipped and fallen at the funeral of the late Cardinal Tomás O'Fiaich. As a result his wrist was swollen and bandaged. But he was perfectly fine, he continued, just carry on.

But Lenihan was not telling the whole truth. He had just come through a nightmarish time in hospital, an event which he had concealed from all but his closest friends and family. The facts about his stay in the Mater Private Hospital in early May would not emerge for several months, days after Duffy had released key parts of the interview he was about to do now with a clearly ill man.

Crucial to the entire saga of the tapes is whether this was in fact the case. Was Lenihan really unable to think clearly that day as he would later confide to his campaign team or did he subsequently use his poor physical condition at the time to explain away deeply damaging parts of the tape?

Once he began to talk Duffy had no doubts that Lenihan's physical ill health had not affected his memory, his recollection of events that dated back more than a quarter of a century.

Duffy's interview swept across a wide canvass, lasting just under an hour. He began with de Valera and his time in office; de Valera and the Arms Trial; how de Valera stopped the attempted resignation of Kevin Boland in 1969; the 1973 presidential campaign; the death of President Erskine Childers; the selection of Cearbhall O'Dálaigh; the resignation of O'Dálaigh; the selection of Paddy Hillery; Hillery and the marriage rumours; Hillery and the Royal Wedding; then Hillery and the night of the phone calls; Hillery and his comments on the New Ireland Forum in Australia; the elections of 1987 and 1989 and finally Lenihan's general observations on past Presidencies.

Throughout, insists Duffy, Lenihan was absolutely open, genuine, giving no indication that he was ill or rambling. He could recall an event in 1966 when Haughey, as Minister for Agriculture, raised milk prices in order to give de Valera increased support in rural areas. As far as he could check, said Duffy, everything he said was accurate.

"The man I spoke to was not gaga," he says, "his recollections on Dev are matched by other Ministers in Dev's Government. His recollections on Childers are matched by others." The revelation during the interview about the phone calls, Lenihan acknowledging that he had phoned the Aras was undramatic. Duffy was so convinced that the Tánaiste had placed the calls that the question was put as a statement - I believe there were eight phone calls made - not a direct question. What was fresh and dramatic was that Lenihan claimed he actually got through, "Oh yeah, I mean I got through to him and he wanted us to lay off."

Duffy then requested other information which Lenihan asked him not to reveal. That confidential information, says Duffy, confirmed what Lenihan had already said in relation to the phone calls. Lenihan had also said on the tape, in a quote that Duffy would later send to him for verification, that after he and Barrett had made the calls he marched back into the Fianna Fáil rooms and announced to the meeting that there was no point in continuing their little exercise as Hillery wouldn't wear it.

Lenihan also, off the record, gave Duffy his analysis of the motivation behind what had happened that night. Duffy will not reveal what it was but he says that his own analysis is based on what senior political sources told him.

It goes as follows: The Fianna Fáil meeting had convened immediately after the vote on the budget. There was an awareness both that Haughey was under threat from party colleague Des O'Malley, and that Haughey had been the first leader since de Valera not to win his first election. Charlie McCreevy had been, just weeks earlier, forced to resign the whip while O'Malley and others were known to be plotting against him.

Haughey felt distinctly threatened. He felt that Hillery not only should be rung and reminded that he had the power to refuse a dissolution of the Dáil but that pressure should also be brought to bear to remember his origins. You're Fianna Fáil, he should be told, we're Fianna Fáil, get that bastard Fitzgerald out and give us the nod.

But the plan was not simply to get Haughey in place and spare the country a General Election. The plan was to make Haughey Taoiseach and then hold a General Election in a position of strength, to give him a quick, decisive victory and shore up his position in the party. But clearly, it would have been constitutionally improper to have done so, effectively dragging the President into the election and eroding his independence.

The interview concluded. Everyone was happy. Neither Lenihan nor Duffy had any qualms about its content, with Lenihan escorting the young man to the door, shaking his hand, teasing him that he had now made him late for another appointment.

Much of Lenihan's equanimity was no doubt based on the belief that his words on tape would be safe in the hands of Jim Duffy. This was after all an academic tape; he had done dozens throughout his career. Academics don't reveal their findings for years and they certainly don't go blabbing about the juicier nuggets of their confidential research. It would be months before Duffy completed his thesis, ages before it was put on the library shelves in UCD and possibly up to three years before anyone outside the hierarchy of the UCD Politics department would lay their eyes on it. Yes, he was perfectly safe.

*

Brian Lenihan had reckoned without one thing: young Mr Duffy's alarming openness in relation to his work. Even before he had exited the gates of Leinster House that afternoon, not one, but two political activists had been told by the student that he had just been interviewing Brian Lenihan. One was a TD, the other was a member of the Fianna Fáil Kevin Barry Cumann in UCD.

Where are you coming from, they asked. Oh, said Duffy, I've just been interviewing Brian Lenihan.

The remarks in themselves were harmless. Revealing that you've just interviewed a politician doesn't give too much away, but it was an indication of just how free Duffy was liable to be, and would be, about the interview of 17 May.

For the next few months Duffy's taped interviews with Lenihan, and former Taoisigh Liam Cosgrave and Garret Fitzgerald were openly on view, peeping from a bag Duffy hawked around with him, the tapes clearly labelled with the politicians names.

Several weeks passed - Mary Robinson had begun her campaign, Lenihan's nomination was a virtual certainty. There was growing public interest in the election.

Duffy, with journalistic ambitions, saw a gap in the market. Encouraged by a friend and the fact that *The Irish Times* had already published an article of his, he approached the editor of *The Irish Times*, Conor Brady, with a view to writing a series of articles on the office of the Presidency.

Brady responded quickly, suggesting that he submit an outline of what he proposed. The proposal was detailed, interesting and quite well written. Brady passed it to political editor Dick Walsh who met Duffy and gave him the go-ahead.

The articles were published in late September, at a fee of £150 per article. Prior to their publication Duffy had attempted to secure another interview with Lenihan but failed. In the articles he decided to use only information that was already in the public arena ie the information that Lenihan and others had made calls but not the information that they had got through. He wondered whether he should name Lenihan as being one of those who made the calls given the fact that the man was running for office but then decided that "historical accuracy meant I should name the people."

Unfortunately for Brian Lenihan it would not be the last time that Duffy would make decisions based on such high-flown moral imperatives. In fact the paragraph about the phone calls was ambiguous, hinting strongly that the calls got through but not stating it baldly. "To hammer home the point," wrote Duffy, "a series of phone calls was made by him (Haughey) and, at his insistence, Brian Lenihan and Sylvester Barrett, two close friends of Dr Hillery. The President angrily rejected all such pressure and, having judged the issue, granted Dr Fitzgerald the dissolution."

The articles were printed and widely seen as good, astute, typical of the academic style of article *The Irish Times* might run at election time. But over in Fine Gael HQ, a desperate team of campaign workers had, they thought, just been handed a lifeline.

The crucial article had been published just four days before the official launch of Austin Currie as Fine Gael candidate. He had been nominated by the party on 6 September and had spent the last three weeks being frenziedly whisked around the country to meet the party activists, who badly needed cajoling into working on his behalf. Robinson and Lenihan had the luxury of thinking about policies; Currie had first to get to know his own party.

In fact the party wasn't quite sure what their policy strategy should be. But two key conclusions in July's qualitative research had alerted them to one possible way they could begin the Herculean task of chipping away at Brian Lenihan and that was to begin to throw doubt on Lenihan's ability to stand up to Charlie Haughey as President.

They had to make presidential independence an issue. It was, said one front bench member, the only issue we had.

The research had shown that 81% of those polled felt it was "very important" that the elected person should be able to keep the Presidency independent of the politicians. Only 7% thought it didn't matter at all or had no opinion.

In their commentary on the findings, noting both Brian Lenihan's commanding lead and the independence issue, MRBI said, "With the very satisfactory positioning of Brian Lenihan contributed to, to quite an extent, by the support of his party at this stage, there is some evidence that a strategic campaign orientated towards potentially vulnerable areas could pay dividends ... One specific area of vulnerability is that relatively few electors (9%) outside Fianna Fáil supporters see him as likely to remain independent of a Fianna Fáil Government (55% of Fianna Fáil people feel that he would remain independent.)"

Fine Gael decided not to hang about. The official launch of the Currie campaign took place in the Shelbourne Hotel on 1 October. A four page statement was handed to reporters, two pages of which dealt directly with the issue of presidential independence and specifically the events of 1982. Thoughtfully, the party had stapled a photocopy of the relevant Duffy article to all the scripts.

The issue was raised in the very first paragraph. "I will," said Currie, "be independent of the Government and above party politics."

After several worthy paragraphs on emigration, political reconciliation, the relevance of the Presidency, the promotion of sporting excellence and the President playing "a real role in the disbursement of Overseas Development Aid" Currie returned to the only issue which Fine Gael believed the public cared about.

"I have," he said "serious doubts about the capacity of Mr Lenihan to carry out the functions of the Office of President independent of Fianna Fáil, and particularly of a Fianna Fáil Government led by Mr Haughey."

He then rehashed the Duffy article (though significantly stating that the President refused to take the calls) and concluded: "It is difficult to see how the habits of loyalty to Mr Haughey for half a lifetime will be abandoned by Mr Lenihan if elected President."

Those remarks, which led the reporting of the Currie launch, attracted a simple blanket denial from Fianna Fáil. Totally untrue.

Fine Gael were pleased with the coverage. They were desperately in need of a boost. Hours after the launch, the results of a private opinion poll to test how well Currie was doing after his whirlwind tour of the party activists, was handed to Mitchell and Noonan. Their man was trailing with an abysmal 17% of the poll.

They didn't tell the candidate ...

Meanwhile Lenihan's campaign was going full steam ahead. One principal aim was to counteract the Robinson youth appeal by moving Lenihan around schools, colleges and youth organisations. No one was quite sure how well the man would be received given the image of the party as innately conservative and anti-intellectual and so it was decided to test the waters. A visit to Maynooth was arranged where the affable, kindly and humorous Lenihan went down very well. Encouraged by this a whole schedule of college visits was then mapped out.

And so, on 16 October Lenihan and his entourage arrived in UCD. A student 'Questions and Answers' session had been arranged in one of the large lecture theatres on the ground floor. The hall was packed, most of the students were simply curious to see Lenihan in the flesh, others had come with a much more serious intent ... Midway through the session a voice was raised from the back of the hall. It was Seamus Kennedy, the then Chairperson of the UCD branch of Young Fine Gael. Did you, he asked, Lenihan, telephone Aras an Uachtaráin on the night of 27 January 1982. No, answered Lenihan, I did not.

Another student, seated in a kind of gallery at the back, had craned his neck to watch the questioner. It was Jim Duffy, hearing his *Irish Times* allegations contradicted publicly for the first time, an incident which he has never once mentioned in all his subsequent media interviews. Instead he has consistently described himself as being shocked and aghast when Lenihan made the same denials on RTE a week later. But why should this have been so, given the incident in UCD?

When asked by this author towards the end of December about that incident in UCD, wasn't it a fact that Lenihan had been asked about the calls several days before the RTE *Questions and Answers* programme, Duffy was initially vague: "Well, I think he was. Yeah, he was. I remember one guy asked him that question from behind. I was craning my neck to see. Yeah, that's right. I remember he (Lenihan) was very nervous denying it. I remember noticing that he was literally shaking. I forgot that completely. Now it's coming to me. I treated it as being an amusing story in effect and laughed it off. God, I thought, there's Brian being Brian."

But Duffy did more than laugh it off. The excited student reacted immediately, displaying once again an apparent inability to keep his mouth shut, telling several people that day that Lenihan was telling lies. He denies however that he also revealed his sources.

"Let's see," he told the author, "I would have literally sort of said, Oh, that's Brian being Brian, and you know my articles. I know what I've written in *The Irish Times* and that it's true, my version is correct. But beyond that I wouldn't have said what my sources were under no circumstances would I have done so."

Asked again about the Seamus Kennedy incident, Duffy said:

> I remember at one stage I was talking to some friends of mine on the Fianna Fáil stand, the Kevin Barry stand, and Kennedy (Seamus Kennedy) came charging over and said Jim, didn't you say that Brian Lenihan made phone calls to the Aras, or made phone calls to Paddy Hillery and I presume by that he meant didn't I say it in *The Irish Times* and they (the Fianna Fáil members) would have taken it that I was chatting to him behind the scenes, and telling him this that and the other and he kept chasing me around all day, asking me what questions he could ask (Lenihan) and I told him in effect to piss off.

But later that afternoon, Kennedy did ask Lenihan about the phone calls ...

Duffy does acknowledge that other people knew about his Lenihan interview prior to 22 October, the date of the *Questions and Answers* Programme.

Asked whether he talked to people about the contents of the tapes Duffy has replied: "There were some friends of mine who knew what type of research I was doing and they knew that I had researched a number of different topics and they knew about my articles and what they were based on. None of them had heard the tape."

On closer questioning Duffy reveals: "A number of casual friends would have known that I had interviewed Brian Lenihan and other people."

Asked whether they had known that he had admitted making the phone calls he said:

I don't think so, I don't think so. One other person probably would have because he's a friend of mine. I used to take his advice quite a lot on the thesis. He would often give me advice on my approach for interviewing and that. He would have known about it but apart from that, no. But one of the things about student politics in UCD is that a lot of gossiping goes on about the place as well so people no doubt would have been sort of saying, well I mean, if I'd stated something about Brian Lenihan in the articles I must have some shit on him but I never told them anyway, nor would I have.

So, on Duffy's own admission, by the night of the *Questions and Answers* programme, a significant number of people knew that he had interviewed Lenihan, other people had been told that Lenihan had been telling lies, that his research proved it, and, at least one person have been given details of the taped interview by Duffy himself. In addition Duffy had already witnessed a public denial of those contents by Brian Lenihan.

And there was one other crucial person who knew about that denial in UCD, Brian Murphy, the former Young Fine Gael Chairperson, now on the Currie campaign team, who had heard an account of the meeting from colleagues in his Dublin North constituency and been told that Lenihan had appeared very nervous in relation to Kennedy's phone call question. From sources in Young Fine Gael Murphy was then given an audience ticket to *Questions and Answers* and discussed with activist Tim Rea what questions he should ask. They decided that Lenihan was vulnerable in two areas - his controversial remarks on emigration, and his actions on the night in January 1982.

Monday morning saw feverish activity in Fine Gael. It was one of the few chances they got in the campaign to have a public go at Lenihan. They wanted to wheel the heavy guns out. Garret Fitzgerald, in Venice, was asked to curtail his visit and appear on the programme. The suggestion was made by yet another former Chairperson of Fine Gael, Dan Egan, and seized upon by the party General Secretary, Joe Kenny, as a great idea.

Also that morning the *Irish Press* had published an interview with Lenihan in a question and answer format in which he had been asked directly about the calls. The relevant passage read:

Q Another allegation levelled at you in recent weeks is that you rang the President in the wake of the defeat of the Coalition Government in 1982, to ask him not to dissolve the Government. What is your recollection of that?

A I wasn't involved. I didn't do it, *not personally* [author's emphasis]. I wasn't involved but there was the option open to President Hillery at the time. It's there in the Constitution.

Q Well, did someone ring him up to remind him of this?

A Someone may have done that, but nobody was going to impose a view on the President. The President was totally independent.

Q But did the President discuss it with anyone?

A I don't know. He didn't discuss it with me anyway. The President was very independent at that time and he didn't discuss it with me.

On Monday evening two briefing sessions were held to prepare for the programme, one in Garret Fitzgerald's home, the other in Mount Street HQ. At the briefing in Fitzgerald's home it was decided to update a statement prepared by the former leader some days earlier once again detailing the alleged events of 1982. A decision was made to attempt to raise the subject on the programme.

Fitzgerald was told that one of the audience plants would raise the phone calls issue and he was urged to go at it hammer and tongs. It was a catch-all issue, raising in one gulp GUBU (grotesque, unbelievable, bizarre, and unprecedented) and the notion of Presidential independence.

Meanwhile out in UCD Jim Duffy was returning a phone call. To Brian Murphy. Murphy had sent word that he was trying to track him down and Duffy contacted him some time in mid-afternoon.

When Duffy was first asked by the author in late December 1990 about his relationship with Murphy prior to the *Questions and Answers* programme, he replied: "The last time I met him in person was during the divorce referendum (in 1986) back in Meath and apart from that I'd bumped into him once or twice or spoken to him on the phone once or twice."

But in a follow-up interview he admitted having telephoned Murphy on the day of the *Questions and Answers* programme, again the following day, and twice the day after.

Both Duffy and Murphy deny that they discussed that night's *Questions and Answers* programme during that Monday afternoon phone call though they did have a general discussion about previous programmes and chatted at length about the course of the campaign. Duffy denies that Murphy told him he was going on the programme, while Murphy says he doesn't remember whether he did or not. Duffy is also adamant that he did not tell Murphy about his taped interview with Lenihan:

> We sort of discussed *Questions and Answers* in general, we didn't talk about the fact that he was on it because I didn't know about it. It was a surprise to me when I saw him there on Monday evening. If I'd known I wouldn't have rung him for a start.

Duffy also had another intriguing conversation that afternoon, with a member of the UCD Law Society. Duffy had information about whether or not Austin Currie would appear at the planned Law Society debate the following Thursday and the two met to discuss it.

During the discussion the two also began to talk about Lenihan, about Duffy's *Irish Times* reference to the phone calls. According to the Law Society member, Duffy then told him that Lenihan's answers at the college 'Question and Answers' session, were at odds with what Lenihan had told him. Duffy added that he would not publish the contents of the tape unless Lenihan continued with his denials as, in effect, this meant that he was discrediting the Duffy article.

When this accusation was put to Duffy he said he was "almost certain" that he hadn't told the student about the tape "unless it slipped out. I'd been rooting around for the tape that day and it might have been on my lips. Could I be mistaken? If I had mentioned it, it would have been accidental."

He added that he might also have mentioned the *Questions and Answers* programme but only in a very general way. He also said he wasn't sure whether the conversation with the student took place before or after he rang Brian Murphy.

Shortly after 7:00pm the recording of *Questions and Answers* began. After a series of questions on various issues John Bowman moved to call on Tommy Morris, one of Jim Mitchell's Dublin West activists, whose question was immediately put by

Bowman to Garret Fitzgerald.

"Given the current trend of indecisive General Election results," went the question, "does the panel think that the role of the President in relation to Dáil dissolutions will change in the coming years?"

In a lengthy reply Fitzgerald spoke of "a whole series of phone calls" to the President on 27 January 1982 without naming anyone.

A row then developed between Fitzgerald and Lenihan.

Garret Fitzgerald: Why the seven phone calls to try and force him to exercise it (his right not to dissolve the Dáil)?

Brian Lenihan: That's fictional, Garret.

Garret Fitzgerald: It is not fictional, excuse me, I was in Áras an Uachtaráin when those phone calls came through and I know how many there were.

A rather tedious wrangle on the interpretation of the Constitution then ensued until Bowman pointed to "the man in the second row" inviting him to comment. It was Brian Murphy.

His question could not have been more direct.

"Mr Lenihan has said here this evening," he began, "that we don't want a President meddling in party politics. But I want to ask Mr Lenihan directly about the events of 27 January 1982. He commented on it, but I want a straight answer. Did he make a phone call, or phone calls, to Áras an Uachtaráin in that period, when the Taoiseach Garret Fitzgerald was seeking a dissolution of the Dáil?"

"No," answered Lenihan, "I didn't at all, that never happened, I want to assure you that it never happened."

*

The time bomb had been primed. Events that would lead to Lenihan's sacking in just over a week's time then began with feverish activity in three separate areas - Duffy and *The Irish Times*; the Lenihan campaign team, and in Fine Gael.

Minutes after the programme had been recorded, at 9:30pm, a call came through to Fine Gael General Secretary Joe Kenny in Jim Mitchell's campaign office in party HQ. The call was from Brian Murphy. According to Kenny, Murphy told him how the programme had gone and, in relation to the phone calls question, told him that Jim Duffy had solid evidence that Lenihan was lying.

Murphy says that while he might have used the word 'evidence' and mentioned Jim Duffy's name, he was simply referring to what Duffy had written in *The Irish Times*, nothing more. It was the following day that Duffy told him first about the tapes.

Meanwhile back in the hospitality suite in RTE, members of the Fianna Fáil campaign team were doing a post mortem on Lenihan's performance.

Murphy's question about the calls was causing no great anxiety. What was of most concern to Campaign Director Bertie Ahern was Lenihan's ludicrous claim that a President would only refuse to dissolve the Dáil "in case of a very serious state of anarchy." He felt that the media would home in on that line and Lenihan himself was worried.

Surprise was also expressed that Fine Gael seemed puzzlingly intent on pursuing the events of 1982. But no one in the group questioned Lenihan about it, taking his denial at face value. Lenihan himself wondered aloud why Fine Gael were so determined to pursue the matter.

The tone eventually got lighter with the campaign group having a giggle at the thought of Hillery and Fitzgerald nattering away and having a jar in the Aras while everyone in Leinster House was frantically waiting for the ousted Taoiseach to come back.

But something was still niggling away at the back of Ahern's mind. Monday's interview in the *Irish Press*, when Lenihan had issued his first media denial of the calls, had unsettled him. There was, he thought, trouble brewing.

That evening Jim Duffy was closeted in the MA room in UCD typing up Lenihan's taped comments on the phone calls. Closing down the computer he dashed back to a friend's flat where he was staying temporarily, switching TV channels just in time to hear the questions asked and Lenihan issue his infamous denial.

According to Duffy his feelings went from "amusement " to "anger". And once again he failed to keep his feelings to himself, telling a friend in the room with him that the Tánaiste was telling lies and he had proof. The friend coincidentally was a member of Fianna Fáil.

Duffy describes his conversation with the friend: "... and after the amusement had worn off I was a bit annoyed about it. A Fianna Fáil friend was there and he knew about my research and I was there saying Oh God this is ridiculous, Brian's sitting there denying it and I've researched this, I know it's true but (it was) a sort of casual conversation like that. But he's a very close friend of mine, he wouldn't spill the beans as such."

Duffy also admitted later that that night in the flat he was transcribing the part of the tape prior to the phone calls reference and that the tape could have run on a bit in his friend's earshot.

The following day, Tuesday, a Fianna Fáil UCD student contacted Fianna Fáil HQ and told them that Duffy had told someone about the existence of tapes in which Brian Lenihan had admitted making phone calls.

Even prior to *Questions and Answers*, on Monday, rumours were coming through from the College that taped conversations, damaging to the candidate, were in existence.

From now until Thursday, it was a race between Duffy's conscience and Fianna Fáil for the tapes.

Both camps moved on Tuesday. On Tuesday morning Duffy rang *The Irish Times* Political Editor Dick Walsh, ostensibly to discuss two further articles Duffy was writing for the paper.

"(There was)," says Duffy, "a casual conversation during which the issue of the phone calls was raised and I just made some joke to the effect that Brian (was) being Brian, in effect there he was denying what was the truth. I think I was actually asked how do you know what you wrote is correct and I made the point that I had spoken to numerous people including two members of the Cabinet at that stage and opposition figures and two members of the (current) Cabinet who confirmed to me and one of those who confirmed to me was the one who made the phone calls. That was like putting it in lights that Brian Lenihan had said it to me because Haughey doesn't give interviews and I couldn't afford to go to Clare to interview Barrett."

According to Duffy, Walsh then told him that the conversation with Lenihan should be made public knowledge, that the proof that Brian Lenihan had lied should be published. Duffy refused. Walsh said he understood his position but suggested that perhaps the paper might interview him instead, give Duffy an opportunity to say that he knew on the basis of his research that Lenihan had lied. Duffy rang off saying that he would consider it.

Duffy then rang several UCD academics including Maurice Manning, Tom Garvin, Brian Farrell and Michael Laffan. He told Manning that Lenihan had told lies and he had proof. He also told him that he was concerned that *The Irish Times* would accuse him of lying. Manning told him he couldn't advise him but suggested he speak to Farrell, Laffan and Garvin.

Farrell was contacted. Suffering from a cold, the normally affable Farrell was cranky and berated Duffy for even revealing the source of his researches to him. He told him that under no circumstances should he release the tapes.

Tom Garvin, the then acting head (now Professor) of the Politics department teased out the ethical issues with the student. On the one hand, there was an (unwritten) ethical code for academic research - on the other hand was someone deliberately falsifying history and calumniating a researcher? It was a very grey area.

Historian Michael Laffan, according to Duffy, came down against publication. He said it was a difficult one to call - on the one hand Duffy had clear evidence of lying and lying cannot be tolerated, but on the other hand the interview had been done for the purpose of academic research and could not be used for any other purpose.

Duffy claims that the net effect of his conversations with the academics was to reinforce his determination not to reveal the information. He rang Dick Walsh of *The Irish Times* again and told him so.

But it was quite obvious that Duffy simply couldn't bear to let it go. Here was a young unknown Politics student, politically active, titillated by political intrigue, with huge journalistic ambitions and now sitting on the hottest story in town.

He had already told fellow students about the contents of the tapes, no one in the Politics department had suggested that he would be penalised for releasing it. He had all sorts of 'ethical' reasons to justify spilling the beans so it was but a short step to going the whole hog and releasing the damning evidence.

On Tuesday morning Duffy had also called Brian Murphy.

He told him that the *Questions and Answers* programme had caused difficulties for *The Irish Times* as they had run a story stating that Lenihan had made the calls. He told him he had solid evidence that this was the case. Murphy passed on the information to Fine Gael's Director of Elections, Jim Mitchell.

Finally, on Tuesday afternoon Duffy played the tape. First, in its entirety, to an unnamed journalist (Duffy won't say who it was but it was clearly an *Irish Times* journalist). Duffy says he did this simply to get an objective assessment of the tape's contents.

The journalist told him that that was definitely Lenihan "in a truthful mode" and that he couldn't have been more blunt. Then, at 7.30pm on Tuesday Duffy played the tape to Dick Walsh and to *The Irish Times* political correspondent Denis Coughlan who listened to the tape and took shorthand notes of the relevant exchanges. *The Irish Times* editor Conor Brady also listened to a portion of the tape to satisfy himself that it was Lenihan's voice.

Duffy then agreed that *The Irish Times* could run a low-key story stating that they had corroborative evidence that Lenihan, Sylvester Barrett and Charles Haughey had made phone calls to Aras an Uachtaráin, but not giving any hint as to what this evidence was.

Denis Coughlan was instructed to write the story. Conor Brady gave instructions that it should not reveal either the existence of the tape or the involvement of Jim Duffy. He directed that the story should simply state that information had become available to *The Irish Times* which comprised 'corroborative evidence' of Mr Lenihan's alleged telephone calls. The editor wanted the claim to be relatively modest and qualified which might appear obscure to the general readership but which would be understood by those directly involved.

He also directed that the story in physical presentation on the page should not be sensationalised and should run below the fold on page one, rather than, dramatically, across the top of the page.

Meanwhile, over in Fianna Fáil headquarters, frantic activity was underway to find out about Duffy and what was on the tapes. Throughout the day, calls were coming through to party General Secretary Frank Wall with titbits of information.

By Tuesday evening they had pieced together a fairly detailed profile - his family background, financial circumstances, family political affiliations, his links to Fine Gael, his contacts with senior party figures, plus other personal details. They had also tracked down Fianna Fáil members who had known, or shared flats with Duffy in the past and who would now be roped in to attempt to flush him, and the tapes, out.

Several callers also told Frank Wall that Duffy had talked openly about the tape and gave various versions about what was allegedly on them in relation to the phone calls. According to one source Duffy had told people that Lenihan had said in relation to the phone calls that "off the record, the boss made me do it," a statement that concurs with Duffy's *Irish Times* article in which he stated that Lenihan and Barrett had made the calls at Mr Haughey's insistence.

Then, on Wednesday morning *The Irish Times* published its story. At 10:30am, a call came through to Conor Brady from the Government Press Secretary PJ Mara. He told Brady he wanted to comment on his page one story. He said he knew about Jim Duffy and the tape and he wanted Brady to understand that Duffy was Chairperson of a Fine Gael branch.

Brady replied that he couldn't confirm or deny that there was any tape in existence or that Jim Duffy had anything to do with the story. Mara acknowledged that he knew that *The Irish Times* would have to protect its source. Brady assured him that the story was solidly based. In fact, he told Mara, people had gone to the electric chair on less evidence ...

Meanwhile the publication of the story had confirmed Bertie Ahern's worst fears that there was definitely something up. He spoke first to PJ Mara who told him he knew nothing. Ahern insisted that it was inconceivable that *The Irish Times* were telling lies, he knew Denis Coughlan very well and there was simply no way that he would write a story without proof.

Then he went to Lenihan. Lenihan insisted that the story was without foundation, that *The Irish Times* had no proof that the phone calls were made.

Meanwhile media pressure on the matter was intensifying. RTE radio's *Pat Kenny Show* was the first to mention Duffy's name, leaked by Fianna Fáil. The *News at One* programme had lined up Denis Coughlan for interview and were looking for Bertie Ahern. The topic had also been raised on the *Gay Byrne* radio programme with Byrne calling for the evidence to be disclosed if *The Irish Times* did in fact have such evidence.

Then, at 12:30pm, just half an hour before Ahern was due in RTE's Dáil studio, he bumped into Lenihan outside the Dáil bar. He had made a mistake, Lenihan told his colleague, his private secretary Brian Spain had just reminded him that he had done an interview with a student some months ago. He hadn't been well when he did it and didn't know much about it but the student had shown him a letter which raised some of the points he'd made in it. He didn't have it but he'd look for it. Ahern was now deeply worried. It was the first time he had ever given two damns about what actually did happen that January night in 1982. He knew he had to get his hands on the letter. Could he possibly, he asked Lenihan, have talked about the phone calls on the tape? No, definitely not, answered Lenihan. It was a general tape of the kind he'd done dozens of times before.

Ahern made for the Dáil studio. Denis Coughlan had been interviewed, calmly insisting that the morning's story was based on rock solid evidence.

Listening to Coughlan, Ahern knew that not only was there a tape but that Coughlan had also heard it. So he played it safe. He acknowledged for the first time that the Tánaiste had done an interview on tape for a student, that he didn't know what was on it but that Lenihan had assured him that it was just a general tape - qualifying every statement with the claim that he was quoting Lenihan. He had no intention of being hung alongside the forgetful Tánaiste. The interview ended. In the corridor outside Garret Fitzgerald took Ahern to one side. Look, he said, man to man, you're in trouble and you're going to walk right into it. Ahern pleaded with him. Is there a tape, he asked, what's on it? Fitzgerald wouldn't answer. Ahern begged him. It's important, he said. But Fitzgerald simply warned him to be careful.

Ahern went back to Lenihan, meeting him in PJ Mara's office just before the Tánaiste was due to leave for a lunch in the Berkeley Court Hotel. He pushed him hard, suggesting that he probably had said something about the phone calls if he had been talking about that night at all. You'd be better off, he insisted, just coming clean.

But still Lenihan stuck to his story, insisting that if he had said something about the calls he would not have implicated himself. Ahern said that RTE was clamouring for interviews and that Mara would have to organise people to go out and bat for him. So they had to be very careful, they had to be absolutely sure that what Lenihan was now saying was the truth.

Lenihan then met with Haughey but did not disclose details of their conversation.

Lenihan stuck to his story and went to the Berkeley Court Hotel for lunch where he was literally besieged by reporters. Word had come through that *Today Tonight* had recorded an interview with Sylvester Barrett in which Barrett would admit to having tried to get through to the President.

Using a private phone, Lenihan placed a call to Barrett, asking him, according to people who spoke to Lenihan subsequently, whether he, Lenihan, had also made calls. No, Barrett replied, you didn't. The Tánaiste, satisfied, then headed off for a tour of Cavan-Monaghan accompanied by Ahern.

Later the Labour Minister broke off the tour in Cavan, driving back to Dublin where other campaign people were still talking in circles, powerless to move without the tape.

By now Ahern had, unknown to Lenihan, obtained a copy of a letter Duffy had sent to the Tánaiste earlier for the clarification of certain points in the interview. He also had a transcript of a portion of the tape containing certain quotes which Duffy wanted to attribute directly to Lenihan.

From the internal Department of Defence postmark on the letter Ahern ascertained that Lenihan would have received the letter on either the Thursday or the Friday prior to Monday's *Questions and Answers* programme even though Duffy had dated the letter several weeks earlier. Lenihan had apparently gone through it crossing off some of the points as inaccurate. Ahern thought the quotes were off the wall, the ramblings of an ill man, but was this really the case?

The transcript read:

On de Valera as President and Contact with Ministers:
"[He'd arrange to meet Ministers] definitely every year, usually twice a year."
"He'd talk about the [Minister's] office, what we were doing, what our objectives were, how policy was going, and so on, in a very general way. He'd add a bit of his own wisdom without trying to pressure you or anything like that. There was no question of that."

"He never regarded himself as being above or apart from party politics. he regarded himself ... as part of the political office of the Presidency, which is a political office written into the Constitution."

On Tom O'Higgins:
"[In the 1966 election] Tom O'Higgins ran a *real* campaign."

On Erskine Childers:
"[We] played down the Fianna Fáilism of Childers ... and played on all [his] non-Fianna Fáil attributes ... a man of culture, a cultivated man, a protestant, the minority could feel safe with him."
"[Childers] - vehemently anti-violence."

On Cearbhall O'Dálaigh:
"Cearbhall O'Dálaigh was a very legalistic man, a brilliant lawyer ... although standing several times for [Fianna Fáil] he wasn't really a politician. His whole make-up and temperament was different. He hadn't got the flexibility that is normal of a person with political training, someone who regularly contests political office, served in parliament, and so on. You develop a give and take, an attitude of mind that's flexible. A person with that attitude and approach, temperament, obviously wouldn't embarrass a Government. He'd temper what he'd say with what the Government's view was. Along with that, O'Dálaigh had a very strong integrity. If he felt a certain way, he'd push for his rights under the law and the Constitution to say it, right up to a conflict point. To that extent he wasn't suited."
"He was an argument for being very watchful about who you appoint President."

On Patrick Hillery and the events of January 1982:
"Looking back on it, it was a mistake."
"A very cautious man ... wouldn't break new ground."
"I remember saying to that group of us, 'Look here! Paddy's not going to have anything to do with this."
"[Hillery] has got much warmer with Haughey since the 1987 election."

On the Presidency in general:
"I feel ... [that] the President should open up an area for himself in which legitimately he can talk as Head of State, in the overall national interest without getting down to the partisan politics, getting down to the remedies that require executive action. That's a Government matter. But on broad principles, where the country's going, the direction it should take, I don't see any reason why the President shouldn't have a say."
"Childers was the man who had the best approach to it. A fellow like O'Dálaigh is dangerous. With all due respect to academics and lawyers there's a danger there because it is a highly sensitive political job ... his [O'Dálaigh's] antennae were not geared in that direction at all."

The above quotes hardly seem the work of a rambling, drugged-up interviewee. What is puzzling is that Lenihan, having received and read this document just days before *Questions and Answers* could not remember, when asked by Bertie Ahern, that he had done an interview with a student. And despite having read the quotes directly relating to 1982, he still could not recall having discussed it.

Meanwhile Frank Wall in party HQ had decided to activate his own keystone cops.

Fianna Fáil UCD students who had formerly shared flats with or known Duffy were ordered to go to UCD and leave no stone unturned until they had found him. Their purpose was twofold: to discover definitively what was on the tapes and to persuade Duffy "man to man" that he should not publish them.

Duffy was to be told that what he had was politically explosive, it was an academic tape and, as he had known ambitions to be a journalist, he would "screw it up" if he was seen to expose his sources and breach confidence.

(Several weeks after the election, Duffy was still being contacted by Fianna Fáil members very anxious about further revelations in the interview. One such member, a solicitor, asked Duffy specifically if there was any discussion of the 1970 Arms Trial in which Haughey had been a defendant, on the tape.)

Meanwhile Jim Duffy had arrived on campus. He had heard

his name mentioned on the *Pat Kenny Show* and had again contacted Brian Murphy, who, under pressure from Fine Gael to get Duffy to give them the tapes, told the student that the only option now was to publish them. According to Murphy, Duffy seemed naively unaware of the political storm he had caused.

At 12.30pm Duffy went to the Chaplaincy building on the campus to discuss the matter with one of the chaplains. The Chaplain assured him that he had done the right thing in revealing the tape contents to *The Irish Times*, that it was a matter of morality, that because a public figure had lied, Duffy had had a "moral responsibility" to help expose it.

Exiting the building, Duffy turned on his Walkman just in time to hear Shane Kenny on RTE put his name to Denis Coughlan in the RTE studio. The young student went berserk, screaming expletives to a passing female student who stopped to ask him directions to the Chaplaincy. She walked off in tears.

Duffy dashed back to the Chaplaincy. He sat down shaking with fright and requested the Chaplain to put a call through to Conor Brady at *The Irish Times*. He was frightened, distressed. By now he had heard that a media posse plus a Fianna Fáil posse were roaming the campus looking for him. They were virtually camped outside the Politics department, had burst into tutorials looking for him, reactivated a disused intercom system in the canteen to page him, put similar messages through the library intercom and had also searched the bar.

Brady suggested that Duffy should see a lawyer. A company car containing a driver and *The Irish Times* duty editor Maev Ann Wren duly arrived at the Chaplaincy and Duffy was whisked off to Hayes and Sons on Stephen's Green who handle part of *The Irish Times* business.

Duffy discussed various options with the lawyer, who assured him that he would have no legal difficulty in releasing the tape. There were three options - he could do nothing; he could say there was a tape, that it was confidential but that it did not contradict what he had said in his articles; or he could publish part of the tape.

He toyed with the idea of issuing a statement the following day to the *News at One* stating that his story was correct but not releasing the tape, a fact apparently confirmed by Fianna Fáil who claim they came into possession of the contents of the proposed statement in which Duffy said, "I do not propose to release the tape as it is for academic purposes unless Brian Lenihan requests it."

Returning to the UCD campus at Belfield, Duffy just narrowly missed bumping into the
in the Montrose Hotel, across the road from UCD, just minutes after Duffy had left following a brief meeting with a friend.

By now, thanks to a UCD source whom Duffy had confided in, Fianna Fáil knew that Duffy had been to see a solicitor courtesy of *The Irish Times* and that he was effectively in their hands.

That night Duffy again spoke to Brian Murphy who again urged him to release the tapes.

The following morning Duffy was back at Hayes and Sons. He telephoned Conor Brady from their office asking to meet him there. When he arrived Duffy told him that he had prepared a brief statement and said he wished to publish part of the tape. He said he believed that it was the only way he could put an end to the persecution he had endured since the previous day.

In later interviews Duffy stated that what prompted him to release the tapes was anger at Fianna Fáil who were using his silence as proof that he did not have anything on Lenihan.

He claimed to the author that if he had held off publishing what he knew until his thesis was published some time later, the contents might have forced Lenihan, by then almost certainly President, to resign.

"I was aware that by holding off I could end up damaging the office of President which I was not willing to do under any circumstances."

(Watching Lenihan's later performances on television Duffy says he felt that "I'd done the country a service.")

Brady told Duffy that publishing the tapes would be welcomed by the paper but that he should check that he was on good ground with his academic superiors. According to *The Irish Times* Duffy said that he didn't want to consult anyone else, that he had spoken to Brian Farrell who had advised against publication but that another member of the academic staff had given him the go-ahead.

Duffy said he would release a small portion of the tape; that portion which preceded the request from Lenihan that certain matters be off the record.

A discussion then ensued as to what would be the best method of releasing the tape, the consensus being that it should all be done in one fell swoop, by issuing a blanket invitation to the media to come and listen.

And so, at 4:30pm on the afternoon of Thursday 25 October, the tapes were eventually played at a jammed press conference in Dublin's Westbury Hotel. Dozens of reporters crammed into a tiny two-room upstairs suite, *The Irish Times* not having imagined that the conference would attract such a crowd.

The tape transcript read:

Lenihan: ...we were in Opposition then, our opposition offices were upstairs....we discussed it ...

Duffy: I believe there were eight (8) phone calls made.

Lenihan: Well there weren't eight, I think there were two or three. There were two or three certainly.

Duffy: But you made a phone call?

Lenihan: Oh, I did.

Duffy: Sylvester Barrett made one.

Lenihan: That's right.

Duffy: And Mr Haughey?

Lenihan: Yes, that's right.

Duffy: Did any of the phone calls get through to the President straight?

Lenihan: Oh yeah, I mean, I got through to him, I remember talking to him and he wanted to...There was no doubt about it in his mind, in fact looking back on it, it was a mistake on our part because Paddy Hillery would be very (what's the word) strict or conventional in that way you know, he wouldn't want to start breaking new gr... he's not that sort of man. The sort of fellow that wouldn't, it didn't, break new ground. But of course Charlie was gung ho. And there is an argument you know under that. We'll have to improve the phraseology of that.

Duffy: Definitely, definitely.

Lenihan: No question about that.

Duffy: It's ridiculous as it stands.

Lenihan: It's hopeless (mumbling) And you see it's ridiculous when it puts everybody in a predicament like that. I mean it's open to that sort of interpretation that existed that particular night you are talking about that's wrong. But Hillery anyway had, there's no doubt about Hillery taking the cautious interpretation. He wouldn't countenance the fact, he was very annoyed about that. I'm a very good friend of his. I know he was annoyed with the whole bloody lot of us.

Duffy: I've heard that.

Lenihan: That's true.

Duffy: I understand from a civil servant that Mr Haughey went to the Aras himself. Is that the case?

Lenihan: I only know about the phone call. I remember distinctly and I've described to you the phone call. I don't know whether Haughey went up himself personally after that.

Duffy, flanked by *The Irish Times* Deputy Editor, Ken Gray and by Eoin McVeigh, also from the paper, was torn between terror and ecstasy.

"Having to squeeze past Donal Kelly (RTE's Political Correspondent) brought it home to me that this was a big deal."

Back at Fianna Fáil HQ no one was in any doubt about just how big a deal it was. That morning, the absence of any follow-up story in *The Irish Times* to Wednesday's 'corroborative evidence' piece had been met with relief.

Then at lunchtime it became general knowledge that the tape was about to be released.

Bertie Ahern now had the horrors.

Shortly after 5:00pm PJ Mara and Ahern listened to a the broadcasting of the tape in Mara's office. What they heard was devastating, Lenihan's voice casually recounting an entire telephone conversation with President Hillery on that January night, implicating not just himself but Barrett and Haughey as well. The two men then went to Haughey's office. The Taoiseach was visibly shocked, but said hardly anything. He simply moved to a window and looked to the sky.

The tape was also being listened to in Fianna Fáil headquarters. "If this had been in America," said one of the campaign team, "we would have closed the office, locked the door, cancelled everything and advised the candidate that the game was up."

The candidate however had very different plans ...

On Thursday morning Lenihan had spent several hours in his office preparing for question time in the Dáil at 2:30pm.

Towards lunchtime word had come through about the planned press conference with Jim Duffy but still Lenihan appeared unperturbed.

At 3:45pm he met with a BBC TV crew in Buswell's Hotel for an interview and then headed out to Sutton Shopping Centre.

On the campaign bus Niamh O'Connor, Fianna Fáil's Press Officer, took several calls from Sean Duignan of the *Six One News* and from *Today Tonight* requesting interviews with Lenihan after the press conference. At this stage no one in the media, apart from *The Irish Times* journalists, had any idea of the tape's contents.

Duffy's press conference then went ahead. Sean Duignan was first to contact the campaign bus, still parked at Sutton Cross. In a voice that betrayed excitement and incredulity Duignan said to Niamh O'Connor "You'll never believe what Brian said on the tapes." And then detailed the contents to a stunned O'Connor. Duignan urged O'Connor to get Brian to come on the programme, suggesting he get the whole thing over with on a high profile show. O'Connor agreed to ask him.

Minutes later Lenihan returned to the bus. In a makeshift office at the back, O'Connor told Lenihan what had emerged on the tape. Lenihan blanched. The man was totally shocked, simply couldn't believe it was true.

By now all three mobile phones on the bus were hopping. No one could make outgoing calls. Eventually Niamh O'Connor got through to PJ Mara, told him that Sean Duignan had requested an interview and that she would advise him to go on. Mara agreed.

The bus was now heading on to the next stop, Donaghmede Shopping Centre. Everyone on the bus apart from Lenihan and O'Connor was oblivious to the drama.

At this point Lenihan spoke to Haughey on the mobile phone. After a brief, private conversation he turned to O'Connor and said. "I'm going to ring Hillery."

A call was then put through to Aras an Uachtaráin. Whoever answered the phone told Lenihan that the President wasn't there. Lenihan then asked for a message to be left to ask Hillery to ring him back.

Lenihan was now ruffled, agitated, trying to hide it from the other passengers on the bus who included members of the McClafferty family from Portmarnock, related to Haughey through marriage, and *The Sunday Tribune* journalist Gene Kerrigan, still oblivious to the political farce now exploding all around him.

The tour of Donaghmede was brief, with Lenihan being pursued around the shops by a hot-footed Brendan O'Brien from *Today Tonight* who had been at the Duffy press conference and had sprinted out to the shopping centre to get the first bite at Lenihan. The Tánaiste simply refused to say anything, and, hopping into a campaign car, headed out to RTE.

Everything at this point became confused. Haughey apparently left for Artane Castle Shopping Centre, in his own constituency, to meet with Brian Lenihan. Ahern too was due to meet Lenihan at Artane Castle where councillors from his constituency were lined up to have their picture taken with the candidate. Then, just before he was due to leave, a member of PJ Mara's staff told him that Lenihan had cut short his tour and was heading out to RTE to be interviewed on the *Six One News*.

Ahern moved, leaving the office to get to RTE to talk to Lenihan before he went on air. As he left he heard PJ Mara talking with Lenihan on the phone. When you go on, he advised him, remember you are addressing the Irish people ... and look directly into the camera, advice that later prompted Ann Lenihan to say in an interview that whoever had given it should be shot.

Ahern arrived just as Lenihan's car drew up. Now was not the time to start shouting at the candidate, he reckoned, best be gentle. The newsroom was like Croke Park with dozens of RTE staff pressed up against monitors to see what would happen next. The entire drama was immensely titillating to all but those directly involved.

A courteous Joe Mulholland, RTE's Head of News, ushered Ahern and Lenihan into a private room, to allow them a brief chat before the programme.

Lenihan told an aghast Ahern that the way to get out of the little difficulty was to go on the offensive, to say that whatever he'd said on tape was not the facts, was not as he recalled it.

Ahern was alarmed. If Lenihan did that they would then have to defend a direct contradiction. Further discussion ensued. Lenihan said that he was quite happy now that he fully recalled the events. He remembered the night, he remembered the Fianna Fáil meeting but, he said, he did not ring the President. He was now absolutely positive that he did not ring the President. Or, as he had said in the *Irish Press* interview earlier that week, "not personally."

What actually did happen, he at last confided to Ahern, was that he and Barrett (clearly under instructions from Haughey) left the room where the meeting was taking place and went into Haughey's secretary's office just beside it. There, with Lenihan sitting beside him Barrett made all the calls but was never put through to the President. Lenihan then apparently informed the meeting that their little scheme had failed and went off to the Bar for the rest of the evening leaving the rest of them to it. He had no idea what happened after that.

That version does seem plausible. Lenihan is known to hate making phone calls and, despite instructions from Haughey, urged Barrett to do the dialling instead. It is also possible that when Barrett got onto the Aras, he told whoever took the call that he *and* Brian Lenihan wanted to speak to the President. This could then have been conveyed to the President in such a way as to have Hillery inadvertently believe that separate calls had come through from the two men. He may then have told Fitzgerald that Lenihan had rung him. When Lenihan went back to the meeting he could have let on that he too had tried and failed. But either way the inescapable fact, which to date Lenihan still seems to miss, is that he did collude in the phone calls. The only thing Lenihan did not do, on his own admission to Ahern, is physically lift the receiver and dial the number. This is in direct contradiction to his statement on *Today Tonight* that he had no "hand, act or part" in the matter. However, much of that was now beside the point. Lenihan did the programme, looking into the camera, as directed by PJ Mara and announcing that what he had said on the tape was untrue and what he was saying now was absolutely correct.

Using a phrase which has now entered the language as a synonym for questionable veracity, Lenihan said that his "mature recollection" was that he did not make the calls. His mind, he said, had not been "attuned" to the Duffy interview.

And furthermore he said, to the horror of Bertie Ahern, he now intended to seek a meeting with President Hillery to verify this.

The effect was devastating. The man looked and sounded

pathetic. Brian Murphy, the man whose question on *Questions and Answers* four days earlier had set the whole thing in train went down to a pub in Mount Street to watch the news. He knew there and then that Lenihan would lose the election. He knew it because the people in the pub just sat there and laughed at the candidate.

Fine Gael wasted little time, immediately putting down a motion of 'no confidence,' citing Lenihan's deliberate misleading of the public, the fact that Ministers Bertie Ahern, Ray Burke, and Padraig Flynn had publicly backed what he said, and the fact that the Taoiseach had branded Garret Fitzgerald a liar in relation to the tapes.

And now, to Fianna Fáil's utter consternation, all attention suddenly shifted on to the Progressive Democrats. The behaviour of Lenihan and of his party encapsulated all that the PDs believed was wrong with modern Irish politics. The tapes affair plus the events of January 1982 smelled to high heaven of stroke politics, cute hoorism, cynicism, untruths, deception - everything that the moral crusaders of the party had vowed to stamp out. Their much vaunted code of political ethics would now be severely tested.

Few commentators initially believed that the party would pull the plug. The coalition was working well, Molloy and O'Malley were very snug in their Ministries, the larger party organisation was still not at the point where it could fight a decent election campaign.

"Let's face it," a PD spokesperson told the *Irish Press*, "this is a painful situation for us. The whole thing strikes at the core of the party's ideology - integrity in political life and so on - but on the other hand the specific issue itself is trivial. The problem for us is how to balance things out - how to continue on in one of the most successful Governments ever, one in which we're steering through the economic policies, and still take some stand on the Lenihan issue. We can't be seen to let them off scot free."

So the party's first act was to let reporters know that the PDs considered the whole affair to be "very disturbing". Party leader Des O'Malley, due to leave for GATT talks in Luxembourg just two hours after the tapes were played, contacted Haughey prior to leaving. He told him that the PDs would have "difficulties" with the confidence motion.

Yet on Friday morning several commentators assumed that while the PDs would spend the weekend wrestling with their consciences, a defeat for the government was on the cards.

But on Thursday night Bertie Ahern had something other than the confidence motion to wrestle with. Lenihan's unilateral statement of intent to see the President was causing him deep concern. This would be perceived, correctly, as Fianna Fáil dragging the President into a political row, the very issue at the core of the entire tapes scenario.

It was sometime after 11:00pm when Ahern finally left RTE after steering Lenihan through a series of bruising interviews and listening to the pious outrage of the stream of TDs and activists dragged in to comment. Having agreed to go on *Morning Ireland* the following day, he finally went to bed at 1:00am.

Ahern now knew what it was like to feel absolutely alone. Much later people would ask him why didn't they do this, why didn't they do that, why didn't they at least have a meeting? But there was nobody about to have a meeting, everyone seemed to have disappeared into the ether. There were no handlers, no morale boosters, literally nobody for the next three days.

Sleep did not come easy. He woke at four, then at five walked down to O'Connell Bridge to get the early editions of the papers. What he read convinced him that the notion of contacting the President would have to be killed. Immediately.

He rang Lenihan's home to pass on the message that he was about to kill the Presidency meeting notion on *Morning Ireland*, but Lenihan never got the message. Neither did he hear Ahern tell the nation that they were no longer pursuing President Hillery. He hadn't listened to the programme and later contacted his private secretary Brian Spain to see if he'd set up the meeting yet.

Later that morning Ahern arrived at Dublin Airport to travel to Cork with the candidate. He was greeted by RTE reporter Charlie Bird and again told him that the meeting with the President was off. Ahern mounted the steps of the plane at which point Lenihan arrived and informed a very puzzled Bird that yes, his staff were still seeking the meeting and he was still most anxious to talk to the President.

So Bird, to clarify matters, played over his taped interview with Ahern to the Lenihans. Viewers of the evening news could see the little drama being played out with Lenihan leaning over Bird's tape recorder.

Ahern had now descended from the plane again to be met by an incensed Ann Lenihan who berated him, telling him that he had no right to make unilateral decisions. Ahern, as always, was stoic, simply took it on the chin and headed off to Cork with the family.

And as Brian flew off, Bobby Molloy flew home, the PD Minister arriving back to the most intense political drama in a decade and about which he had had little time to consult his colleagues. But the media was panting for PD comments and Molloy hurried to the airport phone to telephone a statement to RTE's Galway studio.

What he said then added to many people's conviction that the PDs would not bring the Government down. Though expressing deep concern at the matter, Molloy stated that the party would be "acting in the national interest," a phrase interpreted by Labour leader Dick Spring as meaning that the PDs would not pull the plug.

But he, and everyone else, was wrong. The one person left out of the equation was party Chairperson Michael McDowell, ousted at the 1989 election, but hugely influential in the party and whose views had an increasingly major impact on party policy.

McDowell believed strongly in the maintenance of a separate PD identity, at whatever cost. As his influence increased he had come to be seen as the party's Provisional wing, the keeper of the flame, always quick to kick his party colleagues back into line whenever they starting acting like politicians. More than anyone in the party McDowell could see that the tapes issue went to the core of that separate identity. Even as Molloy phoned the Galway studio McDowell was making plans for a secret meeting that night in his own Ranelagh home.

Present that night were Des O'Malley, Mary Harney, Bobby Molloy, MEP Pat Cox, Assistant Government Press Secretary Stephen O'Byrne, party Press Officer Ray Gordon, plus two party trustees, Paul McKay and Gerard Keegan.

O'Malley listened to virtually identical views being expressed and was last to speak. His clear view, backed by everyone present was that it would be political death "to swallow the little cyanide pill on offer."

He would speak to Haughey in the morning, he told the gathering and tell them that the PDs would resign from Government if he did not sort the matter out. It was a problem of Fianna Fáil's making, not theirs. A view also voiced at the meeting was that the idea that Lenihan should resign could be sold to him (presumably by Haughey) on the basis that he would get a sympathy vote if he did. The meeting decided that Lenihan's resignation would be demanded, but that this would never be explicitly stated in the media.

At that stage no one in the party seriously expected Lenihan to go or Haughey to fire him. There was a resigned acceptance that a General Election was inevitable and then began a lengthy discussion on party funding and who would stand in which constituency.

The following morning Haughey and O'Malley met in Kinsealy for a brief meeting. O'Malley told him the result of the party meeting and then left. Returning to his Dublin home O'Malley again met with the same group of people and listened to Haughey, on radio, claim that the morning meeting had been mainly about GATT talks.

This clear distortion incensed McDowell and Cox who immediately telephoned RTE to take up an earlier offer to appear on *Saturday View*, Cox arriving out at RTE with just minutes to spare. Then and there Cox left no one in any doubt that this was clearly a plug-pulling issue for them and that Haughey knew it.

Credibility and integrity in small things, Cox said, were indivisible from credibility and integrity in large things. Lenihan, in other words, must be hung out to dry.

Meanwhile down in Tipperary, Lenihan and Ahern had also heard the Cox broadcast. Lenihan was unconcerned. The canvass that day was wonderful, meeting huge crowds in Limerick, Tipperary and Offaly.

And there was one other thing which boosted Lenihan's confidence - he simply didn't believe that O'Malley would do him down.

On Monday morning, a Bank Holiday, Haughey's first meeting was with a close political confidante. On the day before the tapes were played this colleague had told Haughey that he had heard an account of what was on the tapes and they were

now in deep trouble. Haughey was untroubled, stating that
Lenihan had said that there was nothing damaging on the tapes.
Now, just five days later, the tapes that Lenihan had assured his
Cabinet colleagues were innocuous were on the verge of
bringing down his Government.

For over an hour the confidante outlined the dilemma the
party was facing. But, as far as Haughey was concerned, the
game was up. He couldn't ask Lenihan to resign. There was
going to be a General Election.

The confidante left just as Bertie Ahern arrived for his
meeting with Haughey. Lenihan was touring Wexford and
Waterford and Haughey wanted him back for a meeting in
Dublin. There was no hint from Haughey that he would ask him
to resign. Ahern promised to have Lenihan in Kinsealy the
following morning.

At 5:00pm, Haughey called a crisis meeting of a number of
his Ministers. At least three expressed a clear view that Lenihan
must step down from Cabinet. No one appeared to disagree.

As promised, Lenihan, accompanied by members of his
family and by Bertie Ahern, flew into Kinsealy the following
morning. The conversation between the Tánaiste and the
Taoiseach took place in Ahern's presence, the two men bantering
together but with the underlying strain palpable in the room.

He was under severe pressure from the PDs, Haughey told
him bluntly. The Government would fall if he remained in the
Cabinet. He asked him to consider the matter but at no stage
explicitly asked for his resignation. It was patently clear however
that he wanted it.

Lenihan replied that he would go into Leinster House for a
while and indicated that he would make a decision that day. As
Lenihan left for Leinster House Haughey went to the airport to
greet Queen Beatrix of the Netherlands, arriving for a short state
visit. At the airport he told reporters that there was no question
of asking for Lenihan's resignation, that the decision lay with
Lenihan himself. His comments were a clear indication that
Lenihan's head on a plate was indeed the price being exacted by
the PDs and that Haughey felt that Lenihan should offer it up. He
also said that the party would put no pressure on him.

In the Dáil Lenihan spoke to a number of colleagues in his
office, including the chairperson of the Parliamentary Party, Jim

Tunney, Chief Whip Vincent Brady, and Albert Reynolds.

Tunney told him he should consider resigning but in a friendly, non-pressurising manner. It was Vincent Brady who got the Tánaiste's back up, telling him that the situation was extremely serious, that the Government was about to fall, and that he had to have a decision now. A prepared resignation statement was also produced.

Lenihan took quite visible exception to Brady's remarks, at the manner in which he, a TD for almost thirty years, a Minister in nine different administrations, was now being unceremoniously bounced out of office by his own colleagues. But the distinct impression he gave his colleagues was that he would resign the following day. In his own way and with no stage-managing by anyone.

Lenihan then left for a tour of the Longford-Westmeath constituency. It was, in the eyes of those who were desperate for a resignation pledge, the worst possible place for him to go. It was where he had cut his political teeth, it was the home base of his sister Mary O'Rourke, Minister for Education. He would be enveloped by the love and blind loyalty of his faithful, and within a few short hours he would be entirely convinced that he had absolutely no reason to resign.

Lenihan's decision not to resign was made on the road to Athlone. En route from Dublin, he was depressed, dejected. He told campaign staff that he didn't know what to do. But then the calls came through. Messages from his constituency, messages phoned through to his Department and relayed to the bus, messages from supporters nationwide. All of them urging him not to resign.

The calls buoyed him. He read them in bundles, collated by his campaign staff. Meanwhile Niamh O'Connor, Party Press Officer, was finding it increasingly difficult to get to Brian on the bus, to find out what his plans were.

In Granard Lenihan had told crews from Sky News and from the BBC that he had nothing to say, that he still hadn't made up his mind.

Ann Lenihan kept guard over her husband at the back of the bus. O'Connor realised what she was doing - persuading her husband not to resign. To anyone who listened she said, "I'm not going to let him resign."

En route, just before Mullingar in the town of Ballymote, Lenihan had recorded an interview with RTE's midland correspondent Gerry Reynolds. He was equivocal, stating that he was keeping all his options open. But the constant calls of support, plus the non-stop urgings of his wife finally convinced him of a course of action.

At 4.30pm, Vincent Brady's first deadline, he had made up his mind. The bus stopped outside the Greville Arms Hotel in Mullingar. Inside he made a speech, stating that he would not resign. He then told campaign assistant Michael Dawson to ring Haughey, to tell him of his decision that he was not going to resign.

Niamh O'Connor then telephoned Gerry Reynolds to come down to the Greville Arms to record a new interview with Lenihan, this time stating that he would not step down. O'Connor was anxious that the piece be recorded before Athlone where, she knew, a team of Ministers from Dublin would have arrived to urge Brian into a different course of action.

Back on the bus the Lenihan family too had accurately assessed what might happen in Athlone. Now, anxious to avoid any chance of his father being influenced by blandishments from his Cabinet colleagues, Conor Lenihan took the one operative mobile phone and hid it in his pocket. O'Connor's phone would not operate in that radius and the other activist Michael Dawson's phone batteries had run out. A frustrated Niamh O'Connor was now incommunicado with base, with the Lenihan family staring blankly at her whenever she asked where the phone was.

Ahern was already on the way to Athlone. But could he be trusted, a man whose chief duty at the moment was to get Lenihan elected President, to twist Brian's arm? Back in Leinster House, Environment Minister Padraig Flynn was told to get on the road and follow him. Ahern arrived at the Prince of Wales Hotel in Athlone shortly before the Lenihan family. At 5:00pm RTE had reported on its radio news that Minister of State Michael Smith had issued a rather premature statement to his local newspaper, the *Nenagh Guardian*, congratulating Lenihan for having stepped down. The *faux pas* further enraged the Lenihan family now fully determined not to let anyone near Brian to pressurise him into resigning.

The scenes of the next few hours were pure comedy with Mary O'Rouke "laying into everyone left right and centre" according to one Fianna Fáil member present and giving very short shrift indeed to Ahern and Flynn. And especially to Flynn. Do you come in friendship or in war, she had asked the two beleaguered ministers. Ahern argued that whatever happened should be in the best interests of the campaign and a General Election would sink all Brian's chances of getting elected. O'Rourke didn't agree, telling Flynn that he could forget any ideas he had of persuading her brother to resign. Reynolds too had joined the gathering, though according to observers his advice appeared to be that Lenihan should stay put.

Lenihan received a tumultuous reception later that evening at a rally in the hotel. RTE reporter Gerry Reynolds was summoned to allow Lenihan tell the nation that he had no intention of resigning.

Late that night Ahern left Athlone to drive back to Dublin. Lenihan rang him en route. He would not resign, he told the Minister, pass it on. Ahern urged him to reconsider, telling him that this would create a major problem for the party. But the Tánaiste was adamant.

At 1:00am Ahern contacted Haughey to pass on the message. Haughey said little, simply enquiring whether Ahern was absolutely sure. He was. Well, replied Haughey, there's a party meeting tomorrow and it's going to be very difficult.

Goodnight.

Earlier that evening, the PDs had convened at 5:00pm in their Molesworth Street office. It seems clear that Brady had wanted to be in a position to tell them that Lenihan's head had been secured.

Shortly before 7:00pm Des O'Malley stood in the glare of the RTE lights on the steps of the office building and read a short statement to waiting reporters:

> Since no final response has been received from Mr Haughey to the point made by me at our meetings, the Parliamentary Party has agreed to meet briefly tomorrow morning to consider such a final response from Fianna Fáil, if it is received.

The implication was clear, the first deadline had been passed.

Now O'Malley was giving Haughey one more chance. He had to deliver the goods, confirmation of Lenihan's resignation by 9:15am the following morning. If not, the debate on the confidence motion, due to begin at 10:30am, would take place in a transformed political landscape. By that time the PDs would have resigned from Government. O'Malley wanted no last minute decisions.

Later that evening, along with Haughey and other Cabinet members O'Malley attended a state dinner in honour of Queen Beatrix. Whether it was a pressure ploy or not, Haughey told O'Malley that clearly the game was up, that the Government was going to fall, that Lenihan would not resign, that it was great pity but that was that. Observers said that the scene was quite emotional. Those who witnessed it felt certain that Haughey had given up.

But all in fact was not quite lost. At 2.30am the following morning, Fianna Fáil TD Charlie McCreevey, a major player in the cobbling together of the coalition deal some months earlier, placed a call through to Mary Harney's number. He left a message: Tell Mary to ring me at 7:00am.

It was that phone call that saved the Government.

McCreevy knew that O'Malley intended to resign from Government before the confidence debate began, to allow the PDs some breathing space and some exclusive media attention before all hell broke loose over Lenihan.

Persuading O'Malley to postpone the decision was crucial to McCreevy's plan. McCreevy had one card up his sleeve. Someone had leaked him opinion poll results, due to be published in the following day's *Irish Independent*, which showed Lenihan now running at just 31%, Robinson at 51% and Currie trailing at 17%.

McCreevy knew how the mind of a Fianna Fáil TD works. Lenihan's low public rating would almost inevitably have a knock-on effect in a General Election. If the party's rating also slumped many of his colleagues would lose their seats. The poll, he surmised, would concentrate their little minds wonderfully. If Lenihan didn't resign, they would, more than likely, sit on their hands while the Boss did the execution. If McCreevy could persuade the PDs to hold off until after the Parliamentary Party meeting, due to convene mid-morning, everything could be saved.

At 7:00am Harney phoned. Do me just one favour, McCreevy begged, don't resign before our Parliamentary Party meeting. Harney said she'd try, immediately contacted a very reluctant O'Malley and requested him to postpone the decision. O'Malley went to Haughey, telling him that at Mary Harney's request he had agreed to do what McCreevy had asked and would postpone the meeting until noon.

Haughey replied that it didn't matter what McCreevy did or did not want, the game was up. His party would meet in a few hours time and would conclude at midday without anything resolved, because Haughey had to go to a state luncheon for Queen Beatrix. Nothing could conceivably happen at this stage to change matters. Well, said O'Malley, he'd promised Harney to postpone the meeting and he'd stick to his commitment.

O'Malley returned to meet his party, as arranged, at 9.30am, telling them that he had just given Haughey some more time.

Meanwhile Lenihan had now clearly gone AWOL. Lenihan had promised to ring Ahern early in the morning to discuss the day's plans. Ahern was anxious for him to return to Dublin as soon as possible. But no call came through.

Niamh O'Connor and Michael Dawson had spent the night at the Prince of Wales Hotel in Athlone. A helicopter piloted by Ciaran Haughey was due to land at Athlone barracks at 9:00am to take Lenihan back to Dublin. O'Connor had arranged with the Tánaiste to ring him the following morning to arrange transport to the barracks. At that stage Lenihan was definitely coming back. He had said so.

But shortly after 8:00am Dawson told O'Connor that there was a problem. He had called up to the O'Callaghan house where Lenihan was staying and was told that Lenihan would not now be leaving until midday. He was refused entry to the house to see him. It seemed that the family were now deliberately keeping Lenihan away from them.

The two campaign staffers were sure that Lenihan was not colluding in this course of action. From conversations the previous night they felt sure that Lenihan wanted to return to Dublin and that he was probably unaware that Dawson had called or that the helicopter was waiting. (Not only was the helicopter waiting but an entire Guard of Honour was standing freezing in the barracks square awaiting their Minister's arrival).

So, to alert him to the presence of the helicopter, they decided to ask the pilot to 'buzz' the house thinking that the sound would remind Lenihan that he was due to leave. And so, in a scene halfway between the Marx Brothers and *Apocalypse Now*, the helicopter hovered noisily over the O'Callaghans' house.

Still no Tánaiste. Dawson and O'Connor decided to make a last approach in person. Mr and Mrs O'Callaghan came to the door. They told O'Connor and Dawson that Lenihan was in bed, resting. The pair were told that they were trespassing on private property and to leave. The door was then shut in their faces. Conor Lenihan was seen at a back entrance. O'Connor and Dawson then briefly considered getting the Gardaí to break into the house to alert Lenihan to what was happening but decided against it, returning to Dublin instead.

The Fianna Fáil meeting began at 11:00am, shortly after the Taoiseach and the leaders of the opposition had delivered their speeches on the Dáil confidence motion.

Labour leader Dick Spring's contribution was particularly vicious, volleys of invective directed against Charles Haughey which even those outside Fianna Fáil found offensive.

"This debate," said Spring, "is not about Brian Lenihan when it is all boiled down. This debate, essentially, is about the evil spirit that controls one political party in the Republic. And it is about the way in which that spirit has begun to corrupt the entire political system in our country. This is a debate about greed for office, about disregard for truth, and about contempt for political standards. It is a debate about the way in which a once great party has been brought to its knees by the grasping acquisitiveness of its leader. It is ultimately a debate about the cancer that is eating away at our body politic - and the virus which has caused that cancer, An Taoiseach Charles J Haughey."

Spring's 'cancer' metaphors many found particularly repellent, given both Haughey's and Lenihan's recent battles with serious, traumatic illnesses.

But as the debate wore on it was clear that Lenihan was almost a side issue. Fianna Fáil were on the rack. The party had been caught out in one final and potentially fatal GUBU. The opposition relished their task, making the Fianna Fáilers sweat over sins that began with the Arms Trial and ended with a voice on a tape.

Meanwhile the Parliamentary Party meeting was not reaching any conclusions. Haughey, however, was getting plenty of hints that if he wanted to sack his old friend of thirty years, his party colleagues were willing to stand idly by. At noon he adjourned the meeting to attend the Queen Beatrix lunch. Lenihan still hadn't been contacted.

Meanwhile the private corridors were awash with distraught Fianna Fáil Ministers all wondering what could be done. Most anticipated a General Election. At least one Minister was so sure that he set about making a deal with a ministerial colleague to fix up a friend in a particular job that was of the Government's giving. Charlie McCreevy was now back with the PDs seeking extra time. O'Malley was angry with Harney, feeling that either she or McCreevy had conned him into giving more time when it all seemed pointless. His vision of a grand exit by his party was fading by the second. Now they would be lost in the political scrum when the debate ended and the Government fell. But, once again, he agreed to more time.

Down the ministerial corridor Albert Reynolds had also met with Des O'Malley with Reynolds suggesting that O'Malley might meet Lenihan at the Dublin Westbury Hotel to allow O'Malley to explain his position, an idea shot down at once by the Lenihan family when conveyed to them.

In fact there was no need. By the time Haughey adjourned for lunch he had heard enough to convince him that it would be politically safe (at least in the short term) to sack Lenihan. He thought it out through lunch.

When the party meeting re-adjourned at 3:45pm Des O'Malley had already been told that Haughey would sack Lenihan if he failed to resign.

Inside the party room, Haughey, after listening to several more speakers, outlined his position. It was insupportable that a Taoiseach could not contact a member of his Cabinet. There was no vote, no clear statement by Haughey of what he was about to do.

But everyone knew.

Back in his office, Haughey put through a call to the southside house where Lenihan had finally been tracked down. He offered him one last chance to resign, telling him it would be in his own interests to do so. Lenihan told him politely that he would have to disagree.

A one page letter was typed up, delivered to Lenihan's private secretary, Brian Spain, to hand to the Tánaiste. Sometime after 4:30pm Lenihan got it. According to subsequent reports, he cried.

Shortly after 6:30pm he and his family arrived in Leinster House, going first to the Visitor's Bar where Fianna Fáil Senator Mick Lanigan wept and Senator Sean Doherty enveloped the fallen Tánaiste in a bear hug. The scenes were wildly emotional, but cut through with bitterness.

Young Conor Lenihan unthinkingly proffered his hand to Des O'Malley and when O'Malley, to Conor's intense humiliation, grasped it, Conor congratulated him on getting his pound of flesh.

At five minutes to seven Haughey rose in the Chamber. Seconds earlier Lenihan had limped slowly in, smiling ironically at the Cabinet bench, neither Taoiseach nor Tánaiste making eye contact. It was an intensely tragic moment. Few who witnessed it were not moved by its exquisite drama. A friendship, much vaunted over the years, and to the political advantage of both men, was about to be ended in the most politically clinical way possible. The Taoiseach said:

> I regret to have to inform the house, that this evening I requested the Tánaiste and Minister for Defence, Mr Brian Lenihan, TD, to resign as a member of the Government and that he failed to comply with this request. Accordingly, I propose to exercise my constitutional prerogative and advise the President to terminate his appointment as a member of Government.

6

The Inexorable Rise of Mary Robinson

Lenihan's sacking devastated the Robinson camp. The public humiliation of Fianna Fáil's most popular politition would do what Lenihan's own campaign team had failed to do to date - light a fire under the grassroots.

Prior to the Dáil confidence debate Ruairí Quinn had proposed that Labour abstain in the vote, an idea which hung in the air for thirty-six hours before being reluctantly dropped. Such a move would have been seen as deeply cynical - an attempt to keep the spotlight on their candidate by preventing a General Election at all costs.

By mid-October private polling had shown that Robinson was on a roll, that given a favourable vote transfer from Currie, she could beat Lenihan on the second count.

Fianna Fáil's internal polls showed Robinson's disturbingly inexorable rise. In August, with Lenihan at a whopping 54% she was second with 26%. Two months later in a survey conducted on the day of the *Questions and Answers* programme on 22 October, and on the day after, she had climbed ten points and was now at 36%. Bride Rosney had always calculated that if they could push past the 34% barrier they could clinch with the transfers.

Prior to Lenihan's sacking, Robinson's 'line' on the Lenihan affair had been clever. Contacted by Eoghan Harris on the campaign bus as soon as the tapes were played, she was urged to take the high moral ground, to say in a statement and in subsequent interviews as she did that "the phone call should not be blown out of all proportion or detract from the decency of Brian Lenihan's record of public service or be allowed to plunge the Government into a crisis."

The same line was repeated over and over again, creating, as Harris knew it would, a 'Presidential' image around the candidate, a woman poised high above the grubby muck rakers in Fine Gael.

But she was worried, and with reason. The sacking had opened a Pandora's Box and out of it came a great wave of classic Fianna Fáil gung hoism as the grassroots finally emerged and poured out their support and affection for Lenihan at monster rallies in the West and in Dublin.

"The sympathy was phenomenal," said one campaign member, "we could feel it right throughout the country. It was absolutely palpable, especially amongst women who kept coming up and saying how sorry they felt for Brian."

A poll carried out by Irish Marketing Surveys for the *Sunday Independent*, after the tapes had been played but, critically, before Lenihan had been sacked, showed a staggering jump in Robinson's first preferences. She would now romp home on the first count with 51% of the vote, tailed by Lenihan at 32% and Austin Currie who was still in a miserable third place with 17%

Ironically it was Fine Gael, who had played such a major role in the tapes affair and subsequent sacking, who were mortally damaged by it. On the day the tapes were played Currie was polling 20% according to a private rolling poll conducted by Fianna Fáil. Two days later he had dropped three points to 17%

But the Robinson camp felt the IMS poll was flawed. Those interviewed had also been asked whether or not they thought Lenihan was lying. Naturally a huge majority thought that he was. But, of course, many of those would also vote for him despite the lies, a fact they were hardly likely to admit to a pollster.

In addition there was also a week to go before polling day, and judging by the crowds that were now mobbing Lenihan wherever he went, a huge sympathy vote could result in a counter backlash and push him into the Park.

The one glimmer of hope, lay in the small print of the poll, the transfers. These results indicated a huge drop in Lenihan's cross-party appeal with the bulk of Currie's transfers now passing to Robinson. Lenihan's tragedy may have increased his appeal within his party, but it served as a major turn-off for the rest of the Electorate.

Meanwhile Bertie Ahern had discovered that Brian Lenihan had spent several days in the Mater hospital's private clinic just prior to the Duffy interview. A hospital contact had rung him and said simply, "Look at the dates."

Confronted with this information Lenihan then told Ahern that he had been in hospital, that his body had begun to reject his transplanted liver and that he had almost died. But he had kept this from all but his family and closest friends.

For several days Lenihan and Ahern toyed with the idea of releasing this information, but in the end never did. Releasing it could have made matters even worse, Lenihan reckoned. The public might forgive him the lies but vote against him on the grounds that he was clearly too ill to take up the Presidency.

And then came the RTE *Today Tonight* TV programme and an abysmal performance by Mary Robinson, a performance which made Bride Rosney cringe as she watched it and pushed Ruairí Quinn into a deep depression.

It was never going to be an easy programme for Robinson despite the anxiety of her campaign team throughout the election to get her on TV as often as possible.

She was weary from the campaign, under pressure with her new front runner status, uncertain how to handle the Lenihan sacking and had just been subjected to a difficult press conference in Buswell's Hotel.

Eoghan Harris has since been blamed for a lot of her problems on that night. It was he who, in a last minute phone call to her home, prior to their departure for RTE urged her to go on the attack against Lenihan. She did just this in a cackhanded, embarrassing way which lost her the Presidential aura she and Harris had carefully cultivated since the tapes story broke. The woman who had said just days earlier that she would not "dance on his grave in any shape or form" was now stomping all over it but in a crude and damaging way.

In fact Harris was not the only one to urge her to attack Lenihan. According to a close associate, lots of people, including herself, wanted to go on the attack, a view backed up by a member of the Labour Party who said that they were coming under attack from their members throughout the country for the 'softly softly' way they were treating Lenihan. On the morning of the programme Ruairí Quinn had gone on the *Morning Ireland* radio programme and given Lenihan a very easy ride, something which had incensed many party supporters.

Robinson was too dazed to appreciate, or care about, how badly she'd done. Quinn was bitterly depressed and ushered her home to get some sleep. "She still kept that spray on smile" as one campaign helper put it.

Now the team was *really* worried. The following day the *Irish Press* printed the results of a Fianna Fáil poll, taken several days after the IMS poll which showed that the gap had now narrowed to just 4% with Robinson still ahead with 43% of the vote, while Lenihan had 39%. Bookies around the country also reported an increase in bets being placed on the sacked Tánaiste.

That night's *Late Late Show* would be the last three-corner TV appearance of the election. Quinn knew that the Curries would put in a good performance and that the Lenihans could steal the show.

But Nick Robinson had had 'no flying time' and there was deep concern about his likely impact on the viewing public.

"Cast in the wrong light," said one team member, "he could come across as an Anglo-Irish Tory."

So Harris went to work, talking to Nick, drawing him out, seeking the 'anecdote', working on the man until at last Nick produced a wonderful, folksy, warm anecdote about the piper Seamus Ennis, which Harris immediately pounced on and ordered him to use.

In the end, Nick was the star of the show. The Ennis story was told and went down a treat, another example of the Harris 'dialectic' of two conflicting concepts in one utterance - the image of the upper class Protestant combined with a man steeped in Gaelic culture who numbered among his acquaintances an Irish cultural legend.

Mary did less well, on the defensive, taking presenter Gay Byrne to task in the interval for the manner in which the programme was going (too political) - a bad move since Byrne led into the next segment with her complaint and demolished it in a rather embarrassing way for Robinson. Once again the ghost of Robinson's socialist past was raised. On *Today Tonight* she had definitively rejected the label and was attacked by Currie for doing so. But this was strategy. Harris had urged her to deny it utterly, not to lie about it but because, as he told her, she was not now and probably never had been, a socialist. Once again it was the Fine Gael vote Harris was courting. Acknowledging socialist links, no matter how historical, might 'spook' the punters.

On the *Late Late Show* she also denied that she had ever said that she was in favour of nationalising the banks. In fact she had, as *The Irish Times* proved the following day by producing a quote from 1982. Unlike Lenihan, Robinson got away with it and she got away with it thanks to the intervention of the Minister for the Environment, Mr Padraig Flynn.

The weekend before the election, Robinson was like Baghdad in the Gulf War, under bombardment from every political missile Fianna Fáil could lob her way. The 'abortion smear' was cropping up all over the country with strange 'family' groupings distributing anti-Robinson literature. In Wexford Fianna Fáil TD John Browne had said at a rally attended by Lenihan: "She's pro-divorce, pro-contraception, and pro-abortion. Is she going to have an abortion referral clinic in Aras an Uachtaráin? That's what I'd like to know?"

What Fianna Fáil failed to realise was that the image of the new Robinson, the woman who spoke about her Catholic faith, her mass-going, her friends the nuns, her links with Cherish, her disowning of socialism, had set - solidified in the minds of the public. The smears simply failed to stick and no longer 'spooked' anyone. The two referenda, though a victory for Catholic conservative mores had also had the counter effect of politicising people on the issues of abortion, divorce and other socially taboo issues with the result that many people saw them in shades of grey, not the black and white of earlier days. The strategy worked out at the start of the campaign for dealing with those issues had worked - she did not deny that she favoured divorce but she stressed her strong family commitments - she openly admitted to championing the right to information on abortion but stressed that she also supported help agencies for single mothers - the Harris dialectic, a core position but superimposed with other images to soften it.

Fianna Fáil strategists knew they had to prise away the Fine Gael second preferences which she now appeared to have mopped up. To do that they had to underline her socialist links and paint her supporters, the Workers' party, as Stalinist monsters. They also had to woo the women by stressing their own achievements in advancing equal rights.

A newspaper advertisement 'Is the Left Right for the Park' would appear prominently in the national papers. Minister for Tourism and Transport Seamus Brennan in a vitriolic attack on the Workers' Party accused party leader Proinsías De Rossa of sitting in the European Parliament with "the old guard unreconstructed Stalinist Parties of France and Portugal," concluding: "It is already clear that if Mrs Robinson were to be elected on Wednesday, this would be claimed by Labour and the Workers' Party as a great victory for the Left."

But then came Padraig Flynn.

Ronan O'Donoghue, the producer of *Saturday View* on the weekend before polling, had one aim in mind. On the programme he had Fianna Fáil Minister Padraig Flynn and PD Chairperson Michael McDowell. This was the first time the two parties had come together on such a programme since the sacking. And O'Donoghue was hoping for fireworks.

What happened went beyond his expectations.

Flynn, instructed by party bosses to go for Robinson on the socialism, 'reds under the bed' angle went gloriously off his brief accusing Robinson of having been reconstructed by her handlers in Labour and the Workers' Party, of having discovered "the new interest in family, being a mother and all that kind of thing. But none of us you know, none of us who knew Mary Robinson very well in previous incarnations ever heard her claiming to be a great wife and mother."

Flynn continued in this stream of consciousness vein for a while until eventually silenced by a thunderous McDowell who, in the tone parents adopt with naughty five-year olds berated the Minister for his attack, told him to have manners, and described his intervention as "disgusting."

That afternoon Bertie Ahern was canvassing with Lenihan in the West. He hadn't listened to *Saturday View*. A rally in Ballina had been terrific with between 3,000 to 4,000 people in attendance, but as he was leaving a woman approached him muttering about Padraig Flynn and saying, "if that's the way you lot are going to behave ..." A short time later, two women Fianna Fáil supporters, both pushing prams accosted him. "It's despicable," they said to an increasingly puzzled Ahern. What was despicable, he enquired. Flynn they said. Ah sure, Padraig Flynn is a nice guy, answered Ahern, totally mystified. Then he went on to Tuam, then to Ballyhaunis, each time encountering irate women, each time pondering how strangely unpopular Flynn was in his own neck of the woods.

Finally in Shop Street in Mayo, a young woman literally grabbed Ahern by the lapels. "It's bastards like Padraig Flynn," she spat, "that are ruining the party my father loves. Why do you let him on the media?" But what did Flynn do, begged Bertie. So she told him.

Later that night Ahern checked back with HQ and heard in detail what had happened. The incident, he told people later, had cost Lenihan between two and three percentage points. The Robinson camp, he knew, had been devastated that weekend. They felt the campaign had run away from them, that Lenihan would romp home. The 'Flynn thing' had changed all that. One prominent member of the Robinson camp puts another point of view, claiming that the tapes affair, without the Flynn intervention, could have lost Robinson the election.

"We would not have won if the tapes had happened and Padraig Flynn had not. Padraig Flynn saved the day."

Epilogue

Would Mary Robinson have won had Jim Duffy not opted to play the tapes and bring down Brian Lenihan?

People on all sides, including key strategists in Fianna Fáil say she would have, that throughout the autumn and into October she had been gaining ground steadily against Lenihan and would have pipped him at the post. Others disagree, stating that the level of transfers would not have been enough to allow her to stride past Lenihan on the second count.

In the end it doesn't matter. On 9 November 1990 Mary Robinson was declared elected President of Ireland.

On the first count she received 38.9% of the vote compared with Lenihan's 44.1% and Currie's 17%.

It's an interesting figure. If it is compared with the Fianna Fáil poll of 22 to 23 October, ie one day before *The Irish Times* published its "corroborative evidence" story about the Park phone calls and two days before the tapes were played, Lenihan was polling 45%, Robinson 36% and Currie 19%. Figures largely identical to the final result. It is quite conceivable that Robinson could have continued to gain ground over Lenihan during the last days of the campaign and beaten him, tapes or no tapes.

The transfers were the key. As Jim Farrelly noted in an appendix to his 1991 edition of *Who's Who in Irish Politics*:

> In the final analysis Mary Robinson was elected not by the Left vote, the women's vote or the 'progressive' vote, but by transfers from probably conservative FG supporters for whom Mary Robinson's chief attraction was that she was not Brian Lenihan and not Fianna Fáil. As they had done in the early 1980's, FG voters again delivered their vote almost completely to a non-FF candidate. Less than 10% of Austin Currie's voters failed to record a second preference and almost 77% opted for Mary Robinson with only 14% for Brian Lenihan. There was remarkably little variation in the pattern across the constituencies.

Factually, Farrelly is correct. In the end it was a 'keep Lenihan out vote' by many Fine Gael supporters and other floaters. But what is crucial is that many of those who either voted for Robinson or transferred on their vote to her must have been amongst those who voted 'no' to divorce in 1986 and 'yes' to the constituional amendment outlawing abortion in 1983.

They were now, in 1990, in the most remarkable *volte face* in Irish political life in decades, willing to give their vote to a woman who supported what they had voted against, rather than a man who personified the old conservative value system.

What this surely proves is that either Harris and others really had reconstructed Robinson to the point of neutralising her former radical liberal image or that a fundamental change had come about in the national psyche since the 1986 divorce referendum. Perhaps an element of both.

And what did it all mean? In an *Irish Times* editorial on 18 October 1990, the writer had stated that one should not seek too many universal truths out of the election. There were good grounds for believing, the writer added, that Irish voters see the President as isolated from other political issues, for example voters re-elected de Valera to a second term of office on the same day that they rejected Fianna Fáil's proposed abolition of PR (Proportional Representation).

"Mary Robinson," continued the editorial, "has been presented with extraordinary marketing skill to appeal to a whole series of constituencies ... it might be said that there is a great deal more of style than substance in much of this. The nature of the office and the Constitution which defines it dictate that this should be so. And there may be more instinctive understanding of these realities in the mind of the average voter than perhaps the parties themselves realise."

Perhaps. But despite the warnings, people did look for universal truths after her election and all political parties took her victory as a cue for updating, even altering, their own policies in a less narrowly nationalistic, more social-democratic and pluralist direction. Dick Spring announced a Labour Party shift to the right, to social democracy, Fianna Fáil announced a radical examination of its ethos and direction and, now that it was safe to take on such matters again, announced that it would produce a White Paper on marital breakdown and repeal the laws on homosexuality.

Alan Dukes was ousted in favour of John Bruton within days of the election. Bruton signalled new party policies on neutrality, Articles 2 and 3 of the Constitution and put divorce back on the party agenda again. Arguably, none of these things would have happened were it not for the Robinson election.

It was not about what Mary Robinson would do in the office of President. It was the fact that it was she, with all she stood for, who had been elected.

An *Irish Times* editorial on 10 November stated that in the past Presidential Elections had had a very minimal effect on mainstream party politics but added:

> This time through a combination of circumstances, matters are somewhat different. The Presidency is non-political. But nothing could have been more quintessentially party political than the campaign which led up to polling on Wednesday. Reputations have been put on the line. Party philosophies have been put up for judgement. Party leaderships have been enhanced in some cases; threatened in others.

The delight in her victory had nothing to do with the expectation of what she would do in office, but rather with the fact that a woman of her political and ideological background (despite the efforts that were made to disengage from it) had been elected.

As another *Irish Times* editorial had stated, the election was about choosing between two Irelands. Electing Lenihan, it said, would be to elect "a man enmeshed in a set of attitudes and values from which this state must escape. The Robinson choice would be committing Ireland to a vision of the country as one which can be open, tolerant, pluralist and generous."

On the night of the first count, when it was clear that tomorrow she would be elected President, the Robinsons went to Bernardo's restaurant with their team. Later, Eoghan Harris, who sat at her right hand side, before leaving to draft her acceptance speech and seek out the words of Paul Durcan "And yet there is nowhere I more yearn to live, than in my own wild countryside, backside to the wind" would write:

"She sits straight, smiling but her eyes have the 1000 yard

stare of a woman who, after seven months fight, sees her destiny draw near."

END

INDEX